Motor City FAMOUS

Celebrity Homes, Graves and Little-Known Locales

STEVE PLATTO

Published by The History Press
Charleston, SC
www.historypress.com

All interior images are courtesy of Steve Platto.

First published 2024

Manufactured in the United States

ISBN 9781467157216

Library of Congress Control Number: 2024942130

Notice: The information in this book is true and complete to the best of our knowledge. It is offered without guarantee on the part of the author or The History Press. The author and The History Press disclaim all liability in connection with the use of this book.

To my copilot, Cris

CONTENTS

ACKNOWLEDGEMENTS

I wish to thank all those who helped and supported me in creating this book, including friends and family, especially Cris; Rob at bookofthedead.ws; the librarians of Bloomfield Township Library, the Burton Historical Collection of the Detroit Public Library, Grosse Pointe Library and Clarkston Independence District Library; Emily Gail; Terry Hughes; Claudia McMahon; Kurt Schroeder; and my coworker Amanda Dalka, who, in college, served Chris Cornell one of his last meals at Northern Lights Lounge.

INTRODUCTION

Most know Detroit as the hometown of countless Motown music legends, from Diana Ross to Stevie Wonder and Marvin Gaye. And they're all included here. But as I went down the research rabbit hole of who was connected to this city, I uncovered a lot more names, faces and places that have been part of pop culture, sports, TV and movie history dating to the early 1900s. For instance, I had no idea George Peppard of TV's *The A-Team* and *Breakfast at Tiffany's* grew up here and is buried here. Francis Ford Coppola was born here, as were Charles Lindbergh and Gilda Radner. Lucille Ball lived in Wyandotte for a couple of years. And the list goes on. By the time I came out of the rabbit hole, I had over one hundred *Motor City Famous* that had me saying things like, "I didn't know Christie Brinkley was born here," or, "I've passed by that street a million times and had no idea that's where Joni Mitchell once lived." This book is laid out by area, using Woodward Avenue as the north–south main thoroughfare and dividing line between east and west. From there, it fans out to the suburbs. Whether a house is still standing or is long gone, I've provided location photographs as of the fall of 2023, addresses and GPS coordinates so you can check them out in person or from the comfort of your BarcaLounger. I've tried my darndest to find the homes of everyone who's lived here, but alas, some on my list have proved elusive: *Twin Peaks* actress Sherilyn Fenn; *The Empire Strikes Back* and *Raiders of the Lost Ark* screenwriter Lawrence Kasdan; comedian Ken Jeong; and *Adam 12*'s Martin Milner, among others. I'll keep digging. In the meantime, enjoy the trip down memory lane, Woodward Avenue, Boston Boulevard and all the other streets that make up this great city!

1
DOWNTOWN DETROIT

ED McMAHON

1420 St. Antoine Street
GPS Coordinates: 42.33732, -83.04178

En route to a fundraiser from Lowell, Massachusetts, to Peoria, Illinois, Edward and Eleanor McMahon made an important stop in Detroit on March 6, 1923. He was a professional fundraiser for hospitals, orphanages and the like, and she was nine months pregnant. That stop was to give birth to Johnny Carson's future sidekick on *The Tonight Show*, Ed McMahon. He held that TV spot for thirty years. He was born at nine pounds, fourteen ounces at St. Mary's Hospital (demolished in 1990, the site was also home to the never-completed Wayne County Jail). McMahon's mother almost died during childbirth, and she and her newborn baby stayed in Detroit for six weeks, while Edward Sr. went on to fulfil his fundraising commitments. Doctors advised McMahon's mother that it would be best if they didn't have any more children. Years later, McMahon would joke that his stay with his mother at St. Mary's was, "Not long enough to know the kid in the crib next to me very much, but we must've liked each other because he cried when I left." This would set the stage for Ed's young life, as the family moved constantly due to his father's jobs. By the time they settled in his grandparents' home in Lowell, Massachusetts, Ed had attended fifteen

1420 St. Antoine Street, at the northeast corner of St. Antoine Street and Clinton Street.

different schools. But it was in that home at the age of ten that he got the broadcasting bug by playing records, performing in fake commercials and reading news from *Time* magazine into a flashlight that stood in for a microphone. It was the start of a long and successful career, which included him serving as the host of TV's popular *Star Search*, the cohost of the annual *Jerry Lewis MDA Labor Day Telethon*, an occasional actor (he was originally offered Bob Barker's role in Adam Sandler's *Happy Gilmore* but turned it down after he discovered the film's overabundance of crude humor) and pitchman for Budwieser and American Family Publishers. After suffering multiple health problems in his later years, Ed McMahon's hearty laugh and trademark "Heeere's Johnny!" opening line on *The Tonight Show* was silenced at the age of eighty-six on June 23, 2009.

DELLA REESE

984 East Vernor Highway
GPS Coordinates: 42.34873, -83.03478

You could not turn on a talk or variety show in the 1960s and 1970s without catching a soulful singing performance by Della Reese. Her distinctive mezzo-soprano voice served her well, both as a singer and a comedic and dramatic actress. She starred opposite Redd Foxx in the Eddie Murphy–created TV show *The Royal Family* (until Foxx suffered a fatal heart attack on set) and the long-running inspirational series *Touched by an Angel*. She was born Delloreese Patricia Early on July 6, 1931, in Detroit's historic Black Bottom district (a predominantly Black neighborhood that was replaced by a freeway and Lafayette Park). As a youngster, she lived on Vernor Highway, singing at her church and embracing gospel music, earning a place in Mahalia Jackson's gospel group at the age of thirteen. Reese attended Cass Tech High School, as well as Wayne State University, before she changed her first name into a first and last name and went out and made a national name for herself.

984 East Vernor Highway, at the corner of Gratiot Avenue, southwest of St. Aubin Street. (It no longer exists.)

2
MIDTOWN DETROIT

HARRY HOUDINI

3977 Cass Avenue
GPS Coordinates: 42.34914, -83.06303

Across the street from the venerable dive bar The Old Miami is what's left of the W.H. Hamilton & Company Funeral Home. This is where Harry Houdini's body was taken after he died on Halloween 1926 in room 401 of Grace Hospital (located at the corner of Willis and John R. Streets, now demolished). A week earlier in Montreal, after Houdini gave a seminar on spiritualistic tricks, a student, J. Gordon Whitehead, challenged him backstage to withstand a punch to the stomach. Before Houdini could tighten his muscles, Whitehead hurled two blows, causing Houdini severe pain. On the train to his next show in Detroit, Houdini continued to complain of abdominal pain, and a nurse on board arranged for him to see a doctor once they arrived. The doctor diagnosed him with appendicitis, but Houdini's "the show must go on" mentality put him on stage at the Garrick Theatre (1122 Griswold Street, also demolished) for what would be his final performance. After the show, he and his wife returned to their Statler Hotel (1539 Washington Boulevard, it, too, is demolished) room, where the pain became so bad, his wife had him taken to Grace Hospital, where he had two unsuccessful surgeries and died of peritonitis at the age of fifty-two. Houdini's body was taken to this funeral home for embalming and

3977 Cass Avenue, south of Alexandrine Street.

was placed in his prop bronze and glass-topped "buried alive" coffin. It was then transferred to Michigan Central Train Station (2001 Fifteenth Street, not demolished but newly restored), where it caught the train for burial at Machpelah Cemetery in New York.

CASEY KASEM

646 West Alexandrine Street
GPS Coordinates: 42.34893, -83.06608

3230 Taylor Street
GPS Coordinates: 42.37015, -83.11420

Kemal Amin Kasem was a born and bred Detroiter, growing up in two homes here with his brother and grocer parents. His unique voice made him a standout at Northwestern High School, where he was the school's sports

646 West Alexandrine Street would have been located to the left of the El Moore Lodge and Residences, where the greenhouse now stands on the northwest corner of West Alexandrine Street and Second Avenue.

announcer, as well as at Wayne State University, where he became the first to graduate with a speech education degree. This led him to opportunities at local radio stations WJLB and WJBK, including the chance to show off his voice acting chops by portraying various characters on the popular *The Lone Ranger* series. Repeated misspellings and on-air mispronunciations of his first name caused him to change his moniker to Casey. He would have working stints in New York, Cleveland, San Francisco and, eventually, Los Angeles, where he got small acting gigs in shows like *Hawaii Five-O* and *Fantasy Island* and served as a contestant on *The Dating Game*. He finally found his calling as the radio host of *American Top 40* and *Casey's Top 40*, which counted down the top forty songs of the week for almost thirty years. He also continued to do voice acting, portraying various characters on *Sesame Street* and serving as the original voice of *Scooby-Doo*'s pal Shaggy Rogers. Ironically, in his later years, Kasem was unable to speak due to Lewy body dementia. Caring for him led to family infighting and several nasty conservatorship legal battles between his widow, actress Jean Kasem, and the three children Kasem had with his first wife. In Kasem's last days, his whereabouts were often unknown, as his wife secretly moved him from Santa Monica to a Washington State hospital, where

3230 Taylor Street, south of Joy Road, east of Dexter Avenue.

he died at the age of eighty-two. As the family feud continued, Kasem's wife moved him to Montreal and then Oslo, Sweden, where he's buried today. While this burial place is far from Kasem's hometown of Detroit, his wife cited her Norwegian descent as the reason for choosing this final resting place.

MARLO THOMAS AND DANNY THOMAS

93 Adelaide Street
GPS Coordinates: 42.34272, -83.05262

457 Brainard Street
GPS Coordinates: 42.34627, -83.06235

On a downtown street named Adelaide was the home of the little girl who grew up to be...*That Girl.* Marlo Thomas was the popular star of the groundbreaking '60s TV series about a single working woman. She was

93 Adelaide Street, east of Woodward Avenue, north of I-75.

born Margaret Jacobs in 1937 to Amos, a struggling entertainer, and Rose Marie, a singer. Amos could not afford to pay the seventy-five-dollar hospital bill to release his wife and daughter after Margaret's birth, so he stopped at Sts. Peter and Paul Cathedral (burned down in 1993) to pray for help. He lit a candle to St. Jude, the patron saint of desperate people, and left seven dollars in the collection box, asking for it to be returned to him tenfold. The next morning, he got a call from WXYZ radio and was offered a job as an announcer for Maytag washing machines for…seventy-five dollars. This is when life changed for Danny Thomas (as well as his name, which he changed so his family wouldn't know he was still pursuing showbiz).

Thomas then headed to Chicago to test the waters as a comedian, leaving Rose Marie and Marlo (a mispronunciation of her nickname Margo) behind at a rented apartment on Brainard Street until he could get on his feet. He did just that, eventually earning $500 a week at the hotspot 5100 Club. In fact, the owner thought he was so integral to the club's success that he offered Thomas partnership in the establishment. Not knowing what to do, Thomas again prayed to St. Jude for guidance. That night, Abe Lastfogel, the head of

457 Brainard Street, between Cass and Second Avenues.

the William Morris Talent Agency, came into the club and told Thomas he belonged in Hollywood. Danny Thomas would go on to star in the hit TV series *Make Room for Daddy*, and he became a successful TV producer (*The Dick Van Dyke Show*, *The Andy Griffith Show*). In 1962, as a payback to St. Jude, Thomas founded the St. Jude Children's Research Hospital in Memphis, Tennessee, where, today, Marlo serves as its national outreach director. Danny Thomas died in 1991 at the age of seventy-seven of a heart attack.

MIKE WALLACE

4863 Second Avenue
GPS Coordinates: 42.35507, -83.06913

Back in the day, it was understood that if *60 Minutes* investigative reporter Mike Wallace showed up at your door, you were in some sort of trouble.

4863 Second Avenue, just south of West Warren Avenue.

After graduating from the University of Michigan in 1939, Wallace got a job at a radio station in Grand Rapids. The following year, he landed a job at WXYZ Radio in Detroit. While in the Motor City, he lived in the Pioneer Apartments, located on Second Avenue, part of the Wayne State University campus. In addition to his reporting duties at the station, he was also the announcer for the nationally broadcast, locally produced radio program *The Green Hornet*. This led him to jobs in Chicago, game show hosting gigs and national news correspondent assignments, and eventually, he became a fixture on TV's longest-running news magazine, *60 Minutes*. He died on April 7, 2012, of natural causes at the age of ninety-three. His death was announced by his colleague Morley Safer on that night's edition of the show.

3
NORTH DETROIT

CLARA CLEMENS

611 West Boston Boulevard
GPS Coordinates: 42.38607, -83.08810

It's amazing what was found in the attic of this home in the Boston-Edison District. This ten-thousand-square-foot home was built in 1912 by Charles Lambert, the president of the now-defunct Regal Motor Car Company, a luxury car manufacturer. After the company dissolved, Lambert sold the home for $125,000 to Ossip Gabrilowitsch, the first permanent conductor of the Detroit Symphony Orchestra (he refused to take the position until they built him Orchestra Hall), and his mezzo-soprano wife, Clara Clemens. If the name Clemens sounds familiar, it's because Clara was the middle daughter of Samuel Clemens, also known as Mark Twain. Following Twain's death in 1910, Clara became sole benefactor of her father's estate. After Gabrilowitsch died of cancer, Clemens moved to Hollywood in 1939, selling the home to an order of priests, the Paulist Fathers. In the attic, they found the unfinished sequel to *The Adventures of Huckleberry Finn*, titled *Huck Finn and Tom Sawyer Among the Indians*. For reasons unknown, Twain abandoned this novel mid-sentence on page 228. In 2003, writer Lee Nelson picked up where Twain left off and finished the novel. The

611 West Boston Boulevard, west of Woodward Avenue between Second Avenue and Third Street.

forgotten-in-the-attic, handwritten manuscript from Twain now resides in the Burton Historical Collection at the Detroit Public Library.

CHRIS CORNELL

660 West Baltimore Street
GPS Coordinates: 42.36707, -83.07671

1777 Third Avenue
GPS Coordinates: 42.33244, -83.06069

Libation lovers, we're heading to a great bar today to wet your whistle for dead rock legends. On a raised platform in the back corner of Northern Lights Lounge sits a red leather booth. In the booth, on May 18, 2017, the lead singer of Soundgarden, Chris Cornell, sat with his bandmates. This was just prior to the band's gig at the Fox Theatre, and the booth could

Above: Soundgarden's back corner booth can be seen on the raised platform.

Right: Northern Lights Lounge, 660 West Baltimore Street, located off West Grand Boulevard between Second and Third Streets.

MGM Grand Detroit, 1777 Third Avenue, located north of Michigan Avenue.

very well be where Cornell had his last meal. That night, after the concert, Cornell returned to room 1136 at the MGM Grand Hotel. At approximately 11:30 p.m., his bodyguard Martin Kristen gave Cornell two Ativan pills, an antianxiety drug he had a prescription for. It has also been known to cause side effects, including drowsiness, nausea, depression, hallucinations and suicidal thoughts. Shortly after taking this medication, Cornell talked to his wife, Vicky, by phone. Based on Cornell's slurred speech and his telling her that he may have taken two Ativan, Vicky called Kristen at 12:15 a.m. to have him check on Cornell. The hotel would not let Kristen in the locked door since he was not registered to the room. Kristen kicked in the door and didn't see Cornell. He then kicked in the locked bathroom door, where he found that the fifty-two-year-old singer had hanged himself. It was ruled his death was caused by suicide, but his family believes the Ativan and other drugs found in his system led to his demise. In 2021, there was a sealed out-of-court settlement between Vicky Cornell and the doctor who had prescribed Cornell Ativan.

HENRY FORD

140 Edison Street
GPS Coordinates: 42.38419, -83.08552

The founding father of Ford, Henry Ford; his wife, Clara; and their son, Edsel, lived in this home from 1908 to 1915. It was during these years that he began his mass production method of making the Model T and implemented his wage-price theories. Both changed the industrial and business landscape forever. They also made Ford one of the richest men in America. From this 7,263-square-foot, ¾-acre home, the Ford family traded up and moved to a 31,000-square-foot, 1,300-acre, fifty-six-room mansion in Dearborn known as Fair Lane, where Ford died at the age of eighty-three of a hemorrhagic stroke on April 7, 1947.

140 Edison Street, located west of Woodward Avenue, south of Chicago Boulevard.

HOUSE FROM CLINT EASTWOOD'S *GRAN TORINO*

238 Rhode Island Street
GPS Coordinates: 42.40026, -83.08329

"Go ahead, make my day." "Do you feel lucky? Well, do you, punk?" "Get off my lawn." On paper in a script, lines like these may not immediately jump off the page. But when uttered by Clint Eastwood in a movie, they almost instantly become T-shirt-worthy. "Get off my lawn," was uttered by him in front of this two-story home in the 2008 film *Gran Torino*. The interiors were also shot here. And the interior and exterior of the Vang Lor house next door at 234 Rhode Island Street were also used. The story was originally set in Minneapolis, but Eastwood thought that since his character was a retired auto worker, the film should be set and shot in Detroit. It was also the first movie to take advantage of Michigan's new (and now-defunct) liberal incentive package offered to Hollywood, of which this film received a 42 percent tax credit. The movie was shot in July 2008 and was a hit when released during Christmas that year. Ultimately, *Gran Torino* became the tenth-highest-grossing Clint Eastwood movie of all time.

KIM HUNTER

427 Highland Street
GPS Coordinates: 42.39279, -83.10521

One of the most indelible scenes and lines from a movie comes from a drunk Marlon Brando when he grips the sides of his head and yells "Stella!" up to a neighbor's apartment, where his beaten wife has sought refuge from him. The movie was *A Streetcar Named Desire*, and Stella was played by Kim Hunter. This role earned her an Oscar and Golden Globe Award for Best Supporting Actress. She was born Janet Cole in 1922 and lived on Highland Street until her engineer father died in 1926 and her concert pianist mother remarried and relocated to Miami. When the Lodge Freeway was built in three sections during the 1950s and 1960s, the freeway went right through the site where their house once stood. Her name change came when RKO Pictures signed her to a seven-year contract. Movie mogul David O. Selznick suggested

238 Rhode Island Street, located east of Woodward Avenue, south of the Davison Freeway.

427 Highland Street, located south of the Davison Freeway, east of the Lodge Freeway.

Kim for a first name, and his secretary suggested Hunter for a last name. She was a founding member of the Actor's Studio and found her way onto McCarthy's blacklist in the 1950s. But afterward, her career miraculously endured, with her having memorable performances in everything from Rod Serling's *Requiem for a Heavyweight* to the soap opera staple *The Edge of Night* and the disturbing TV movie *Bad Ronald*, in which she played a mom who kept her son under the stairway. But perhaps the role she's most well-known for is the one for which she underwent four and a half hours of prosthetic makeup to play chimpanzee psychologist and veterinarian Dr. Zira in the first three original *Planet of the Apes* films. Hunter died of a heart attack at the age of seventy-nine on September 11, 2002.

JAMES LIPTON

280 Hague Street
GPS Coordinates: 42.38017, -83.07533

"What is your favorite curse word?" "What sound or noise do you hate?" "What profession would you not like to do?" Those were some of the questions *Inside the Actor's Studio* host James Lipton posed to countless thespians who appeared on his long-running interview show. Where was he born, you ask?

280 Hague Street, located east of Woodward Avenue, north of East Grand Boulevard.

Detroit's North End. He lived here with his mother (his father abandoned the family when he was young) on Hague Street. After graduating from Central High School, he landed the part of the Lone Ranger's nephew Dan Reid on the wildly popular WXYZ radio show *The Lone Ranger*. He attended Wayne State University briefly before he joined the air force, and then he moved to New York City. There, he went on to other acting gigs and became a TV writer, lyricist, author, producer and a parodied-by-Will-Ferrell character on *Saturday Night Live*. If heaven exists, Lipton arrived there on March 2, 2020, after he succumbed to bladder cancer at the age of ninety-three.

HARRY MORGAN

198 Rhode Island Street
GPS Coordinates: 42.39976, -83.08459

Ten houses down from the house where Clint Eastwood filmed *Gran Torino* is the house where actor Harry Morgan was born. It makes you wonder if Eastwood knew he was that close to Morgan's birthplace, the home of someone whom Eastwood had once appeared with, uncredited, in a movie, 1956's *Star in the Dust*. It was Eastwood's first western. Morgan lived here for a short time before his family moved to Muskegon, Michigan. He had roles

198 Rhode Island Street, located east of Woodward Avenue, south of the Davison Freeway.

in countless movies, including *The Ox-bow Incident*, *High Noon* and *The Apple Dumpling Gang*, but TV was where he was known best. He played Colonel Sherman T. Potter on *M*A*S*H** (1975–83) and Joe Gannon on *Dragnet* (1967–70). Morgan died in 2011 from pneumonia at the age of ninety-six.

GEORGE PEPPARD

99 Burlingame Street
GPS Coordinates: 42.39125, -83.08949

710 North Waverly Street
GPS Coordinates: 42.31637, -83.26981

Northview Cemetery
23755 Military Road, Dearborn Heights
GPS Coordinates: 42.31602, -83.25694

George Peppard was born and buried here in Detroit. And in between, he was one of Hollywood's most popular actors. Peppard's breakout role was starring opposite Audrey Hepburn in *Breakfast at Tiffany's*. And later in life, he gained fame with a new generation of fans starring opposite Mr. T in TV's

Opposite: 710 North Waverly Street, located east of Telegraph Road, north of Michigan Avenue.

Right: 99 Burlingame Street, located west of Woodward Avenue, south of the Davison Freeway.

Below: Northview Cemetery, 23755 Military Road, located east of Outer Drive, north of Cherry Hill Road. Enter through gates at the end of Kensington Street, follow the road to right and continue parallel to Outer Drive. The headstone is on the right at the roadside, about a third of the way down the road.

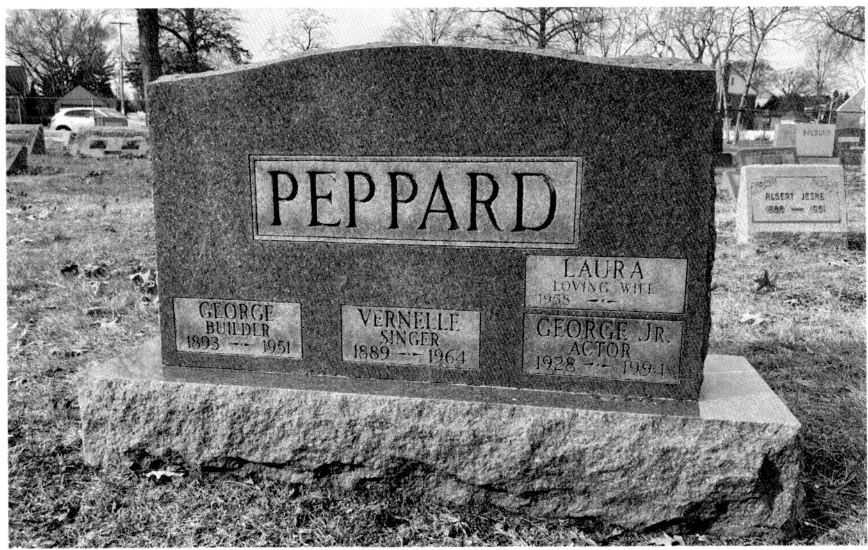

The A-Team. Born on Burlingame Street in Detroit, he grew up in Dearborn, where he graduated from Dearborn High School in 1946. He went to Purdue University to study engineering but transferred to Carnegie Mellon, where he took up acting and joined the Actor's Studio. Peppard went on to star in *The Carpetbaggers*, *How the West Was Won* and as TV's *Banacek*. After smoking three packs of cigarettes a day for most of his life, he died at the age of sixty-five of pneumonia while battling lung cancer. As was his wish, he was buried in his hometown with his family at Northview Cemetery.

SMOKEY ROBINSON

581 Belmont Street
GPS Coordinates: 42.39168, -83.07827

17077 Westland Avenue
GPS Coordinates: 42.44809, -83.21141

If you asked a young William Robinson what he wanted to be when he grew up, he would have told you he wanted to be a cowboy. His uncle Claude would take him to see every Gene Autry and Roy Rogers movie that came out, so he made up a cowboy-sounding nickname for Robinson: Smokey Joe. It stuck until Robinson was around the age of twelve, when he dropped the "Joe." Smokey Robinson grew up on Belmont Street, just seven houses down from Diana Ross's childhood home. In 1955, while he was a student at Northern Senior High School, Robinson and his friends formed a singing group, The Five Chimes, that was later renamed The Matadors. After a couple of years, they were good enough to begin playing Detroit clubs, and with the addition of Smokey's soon-to-be wife and future ex-wife, Claudette Robinson, they changed their name to The Miracles. In 1959, they were one of the first groups to be signed to Motown Records. A year later, they released megahit "Shop Around," and the group skyrocketed to fame. In 1965, Berry Gordy made the decision to change the group's name for the final time to Smokey Robinson and the Miracles. The thought was that they could charge more with an individual name out in front of the group name because it was seen as more of a personal appearance. Their performance fee increased five times with this change. They had hit after hit throughout the 1960s and into the early 1970s. Tired of life on the road

Above: 581 Belmont Street, located east of Woodward Avenue, north of Arden Park Boulevard.

Right: Diana Ross's childhood home, 635 Belmont Street.

Northern Senior High School, located at Woodward Avenue and Owen Street.

17077 Westland Avenue, located east of Southfield Road, north of 8 Mile Road.

and wanting to settle down with his family, Robinson bought a mid-century modern home on Westland Avenue, where he lived from 1970 to 1972, until Motown headed to Los Angeles to add movies and TV to its music empire. Robinson followed, striking out on his own as a successful solo act with hits like "Cruisin'" and "Being with You."

4
WEST DETROIT

TY COBB

4117 Commonwealth Street
GPS Coordinates: 42.34561, -83.07672

800 Atkinson Street
GPS Coordinates: 42.38183, -83.08869

Ty Cobb was not going to win any Mr. Congeniality awards. But of this legendary Detroit Tigers center fielder, Babe Ruth once said, "Sure, Cobb's a prick, but God Almighty, that old man can still hit and run." Cobb was known to have a short fuse and was said to be combative with teammates, ornery with stadium staff and a drinker, all of which have added to the myth of Ty Cobb. But truth be told, much of this was designed to keep members of the opposing team off-balance and psyched out. Cobb was a perfectionist and expected his teammates to play to their highest level. He joined the Tigers from a semiprofessional league in Atlanta in August 1905, the same month his mother shot and killed his father, whom Cobb called "the greatest man I ever knew." What actually occurred has been a source of debate, but in the end, Cobb's mother was charged with murder and acquitted, and it affected Cobb for the rest of his life. A grieving Cobb moved to Detroit with his wife, Charlie, and their son, Ty Jr., and they lived on the right side of a duplex on Commonwealth Street for three years,

4117 Commonwealth Street, located west of Trumbull Street, east of West Grand River Avenue.

800 Atkinson Street, located west of Woodward Avenue, south of Chicago Boulevard.

arguably his greatest as a ballplayer. His daughter, Shirley, was born in this home, and he'd often walk his dogs down Trumbull Street to play a game at Bennett Park (later Navin Field, Briggs Stadium and Tiger Stadium). He was repeatedly on the list of the highest-paid baseball players and was a shrewd investor. Eventually, the Cobbs moved to Atkinson Street in the upscale Boston-Edison District. When Cobb retired as a player in 1928, he held career records for games played (3,305), at-bats (2,246), hits (4,189 or 4,191, depending on the source), total bases (5,854) and batting average (.367 or .366, depending on the source). Cobb died in Atlanta at the age of seventy-four of prostate cancer on July 17, 1961.

TONY HAWK

3966 Trumbull Street
GPS Coordinates: 42.34554, -83.07450

Tony Hawk, the skateboarding phenom known as "Birdman," landed this late-1800s Second Empire–style home in the Woodbridge neighborhood of Detroit. It was once the home of Trumbull General Hospital in the 1940s until it closed in 1974. It was abandoned until 2011, when it was bought and turned into three 1,200-square-foot apartments. Hawk was a frequent visitor

3966 Trumbull Street, located north of West Grand River Avenue.

to Detroit, as his fourth wife was raised here; his The Skatepark Project constructed the Chandler Park Skatepark here; and he founded D/CAL, a marketing firm based here and in California. Hawk bought this building in 2016, renting out two of the apartments and keeping one for himself for his visits to Detroit.

CHARLES LINDBERGH

1120 West Forest Avenue
GPS Coordinates: 42.35195, -83.07419

945 Cranbrook Road
GPS Coordinates: 42.57487, -83.24161

If pioneering aviator Charles Lindbergh was alive today and able to fly over his birthplace, he'd look down and find the Freedom Place Apartments complex. He was born here on West Forest Avenue on February 4, 1902. A plaque out front used to mark the historical home, but on July 24, 1972, the interior of the home was destroyed by fire, and the property was demolished. The plaque was never replaced. This was not the only time Lindbergh lived in the Detroit area. In 1942, Henry

1120 West Forest Avenue, now the site of the Freedom Place Apartments, located west of the Lodge Freeway, east of Trumbull Street.

945 North Cranbrook Road, located west of Woodward, south of Long Lake Road.

Ford invited him to work as a consultant in retooling his Willow Run facility to go from auto manufacturing to bomber production. Ford put up Lindbergh and his wife, author Anne Morrow Lindbergh, in the fully furnished Albert Kahn–designed Stonelea (now the Lyon House) at the entrance to the Cranbrook Educational Community in Bloomfield Hills. The Lindberghs lived here for one year.

DICK MARTIN

2540 Central Street
GPS Coordinates: 42.31541, -83.12571

You bet your sweet bippy Dick Martin lived here. He was born Thomas Richard Martin in Battle Creek on January 30, 1922, but was raised in Detroit. We know him as the funny half of the comedy team who helmed TV's *Rowan & Martin's Laugh-In*, which ran from 1968 to 1972. The show broke TV barriers with its risqué humor and political skewering and was a launching pad for many comedians, including fellow Detroiter Lily Tomlin. Martin teamed with Dan Rowan in 1952 but broke away for a year to play

2540 Central Street, Apartment D2 (located on the left side of the building), between Vernor Highway and Dix Highway.

Lucille Ball's neighbor on her second sitcom *The Lucy Show*. After Rowan retired in the early '80s, Martin made numerous appearances on game shows and directed sitcoms from *The Nanny* to *Newhart*, including its last episode, considered by many to be the greatest ending to a TV show ever. He died on May 24, 2008, at the age of eighty-six from breathing complications brought on by the lifelong effects of tuberculosis, which he suffered from as a teenager in Detroit.

SIXTO RODRIGUEZ

4820 Avery Street
GPS Coordinates: 42.35091, -83.08053

Holy Cross Cemetery
8850 Dix Avenue
GPS Coordinates: 42.31604, -83.14088

If it wasn't for the Oscar-winning documentary *Searching for Sugarman*, many may never have even heard of the tremendously talented Sixto

4820 Avery Street, located south of West Warren Avenue, between Trumbull Street and Rosa Parks Boulevard.

Holy Cross Cemetery, located at 8850 Dix Avenue, between I-94 and I-75. Section S, lot 5, grave 798, located on the far-left side of the cemetery, along the back fence. As of this publication, his engraved headstone has not been placed.

Rodriguez. Though he was not widely known in the United States prior to the film's release, he was big in New Zealand, South Africa and Australia, reportedly outselling Elvis. The subject of the documentary concerned the incorrect rumor that Rodriguez had died and the search to find out what happened to him. He was found alive and well, living in this house in Detroit's Woodbridge neighborhood. The success of the documentary reintroduced Rodriguez to a whole new (as well as old) audience, and he toured until the COVID-19 pandemic hit. Despite his newfound fame, Rodriguez remained in this house, which he bought at a government auction for fifty dollars. He lived here until he died from complications of a stroke at the age of eighty-one on August 8, 2023, and was buried in Holy Cross Cemetery.

JACK WHITE

1203 Ferdinand Street
GPS Coordinates: 42.31419, -83.09640

1731 Seminole Street
GPS Coordinates: 42.35815, -82.99656

Had their paths not crossed one night in Royal Oak, the duo that made up The White Stripes may have wound up as a chef and an upholsterer or priest. Jack Gillis grew up on Ferdinand Street in Mexicantown, the youngest of ten kids. He was accepted to a seminary school in Wisconsin but instead went to Cass Tech High School and took a job as an apprentice upholsterer. Meg White worked at Memphis Smoke (at 11 Mile Road and Main Street; it has been many restaurants since) as a bartender with ambitions to become a chef. The two met when Jack read poetry there, and they were married in 1996, with Jack taking her last name. This was all before they formed their influential garage rock band, as it wasn't until Meg picked up a pair of drumsticks that the idea for the band materialized. They began playing local venues, presenting themselves as a brother and sister to have the focus be more naturally on the music, not a husband and wife coming together to form a contrived band. They divorced in 2000 but kept the band together and made it big, winning six Grammy Awards, five MTV Video Music Awards and a nomination into the Rock and Roll

Top: 1203 Ferdinand Street, located north of I-75, west of Clark Avenue.

Bottom: 1731 Seminole Street, east of Van Dyke Avenue, south of Kercheval.

Hall of Fame in 2023. With the band's success, Jack moved to this Indian Village home on Seminole Street and lived here from 2001 to 2007. The White Stripes called it quits in 2011.

5
EAST DETROIT

LIZZO

295 Hague Street
GPS Coordinates: 42.38061, -83.07528

12012 Northlawn Street
GPS Coordinates: 42.37634, -83.15240

5800 Bishop Street
GPS Coordinates: 42.41145, -82.93703

16743 Chandler Park Drive
GPS Coordinates: 42.41024, -82.93673

A music superstar-to-be named Melissa Viviane Jefferson was born at Hutzel Women's Hospital on April 27, 1988. She is the youngest of the three Jefferson kids after her sister, Vanessa, and brother, Mikey. The girl who would take the music world by storm and her family lived in several homes in the Detroit area before they moved to Houston, Texas, when she was about ten years old. There, around the age of fourteen, she earned the nickname Lizzo, which is a riff on Lissa (short for Melissa) mashed up with Jay-Z's song title "Izzo (H.O.V.A.)." Needless to say, the name stuck. Superstardom came her way after recording hits like "Truth Hurts," "About Damn Time" and "Tempo."

295 Haguc Street, located east of Woodward Avenue, south of Holbrook Avenue. (It no longer exists.)

12012 Northlawn Street, located north of Grand River Avenue, west of I-96.

5800 Bishop Street, located southeast of I-94, east of Outer Drive East, just a few houses down from the Chandler Park Drive home.

16743 Chandler Park Drive, located southeast of I-94, east of Outer Drive East.

MARTHA REEVES

2409 Townsend Street
GPS Coordinates: 42.35929, -83.00565

16170 La Salle Avenue
GPS Coordinates: 42.41143, -83.12506

Martha Reeves came to Detroit when she was just a baby, living on Townsend Street and attending Metropolitan Church, where her grandfather was the minister. She grew up singing in the choir, and after she graduated from Northeastern High School, she took odd jobs during the day and nightclub gigs at night. One of those gigs was attended by a scout for Motown Records who invited her to make an appointment for an audition. Instead, she showed up unannounced, which resulted in her being asked to answer phones. Martha ended up being a combination secretary and demo recorder, until one day, when backing vocals were needed for Marvin Gaye, she and her singing friends stepped in. With that, Martha and the Vandellas (the name was a combination of Van Dyke, the street, and her

2409 Townsend Street, located north of East Vernor Highway, east of East Grand Boulevard.

16170 La Salle Avenue, located between West McNichols Highway and Puritan Avenue.

favorite singer, Della Reese) were signed to Motown. They would go on to deliver hit after hit, from "Dancin' in the Streets" and "Nowhere to Run" to "Heat Wave" and "Jimmy Mack." During her heyday, Reeves bought a home on La Salle Avenue, where many Motown artists resided. In the early '70s, when Hitsville USA hit the road to Los Angeles, Reeves embarked on a solo career and reteamed with the Vandellas on various occasions, including at their induction into the Rock and Roll Hall of Fame in 1995. Reeves has performed at the Super Bowl, been a musical guest on the first season of *Saturday Night Live* and even served on the Detroit City Council from 2005 to 2009.

6

NORTHWEST DETROIT

AALIYAH

19315 Warrington Drive
GPS Coordinates: 42.43488, -83.14060

One of the more tragic stories to come out of Detroit is that of the young R&B singer/actress Aaliyah Haughton, who grew up in the idyllic Sherwood Forest area of the city. She sang at her church, acted in plays at Gesu Elementary School and joined her aunt Gladys Knight on stage when she toured. At the age of ten, she appeared on *Star Search* and auditioned for TV roles and commercials. Despite Aaliyah's talent, her manager, Barry Hankerson (Knight's ex-husband and Aaliyah's uncle), could not get a major label to sign her. At the time, Hankerson was also R. Kelly's manager, and he leaned on Kelly to help get Aaliyah a contract with Jive, the label for such superstars as the Backstreet Boys, NSYNC and Britany Spears. Aaliyah got the contract, but it came with the notorious Kelly as the executive producer and writer on the then-fourteen-year-old's debut album, *Age Ain't Nothin' but a Number*. Rumors about their relationship had been circulating for some time, and when he was twenty-seven, Kelly secretly wed fifteen-year-old Aaliyah, though the marriage certificate stated her age as eighteen. When her father learned of their marriage the next year, he forced it to be annulled. A nondisclosure agreement between

19315 Warrington Drive, located north of 7 Mile Road, east of Livernois Avenue.

Kelly and Aaliyah kept things quiet, but in 2023, the law caught up with Kelly for the years he sexually abused underage girls, and he was sentenced to twenty years in prison. Despite this part of her life, Aaliyah flourished as a young student, R&B singer and actress. She graduated from the Detroit High School for the Fine and Performing Arts with a 4.0 GPA, was nominated for five Grammy Awards, won three American Music Awards and two MTV Video Awards and starred in the films *Romeo Must Die* and *Queen of the Damned*. On August 25, 2001, she wrapped shooting early in the Bahamas for her "Rock the Boat" video. Anxious to leave, she and seven of her crew members chartered a plane to Miami, which had one too many passengers and was seven hundred pounds over its weight limit. The plane crashed on takeoff, killing the pilot and all passengers, including the twenty-two-year-old Aaliyah.

BIG SEAN

18011 Northlawn Street
GPS Coordinates: 42.42285, -83.15424

This was the boyhood home of Sean Anderson, who moved to Detroit from Santa Monica, California, when he was three months old. Raised by his mother and grandmother, he attended Detroit Waldorf School and is yet another famous graduate of Cass Tech High School. During his high school years, he participated in weekly rap battles at the hip-hop station WHTD, where, one day, over the air, he heard that Kanye West was doing an interview at 102.7 FM. He raced over to the station, freestyle rapped for West and handed him a demo tape. Two years later, he was signed to West's GOOD Music label. Of his stage name, Anderson said that when he was young, there was a six-foot-eight guy in the neighborhood who was also named Sean, who was a role model for him. Anderson, being much shorter, jokingly insisted he should be called "Big Sean" and that his taller mentor should be called "Little Sean." Big Sean has gone on to become an accomplished, award-winning rapper on his own and when collaborating

18011 Northlawn Street, located east of the Lodge Freeway, north of West McNichols Road.

with the likes of Eminem, Lil Wayne and Travis Scott. He has also been a big promotor of Detroit, through both his music and his Sean Anderson Foundation, which helps underserved children and families of the city in numerous ways.

ELLEN BURSTYN

3271 and 3277 Hazelwood Street
GPS Coordinates: 42.36895, -83.11418 & 42.36892, -83.11425

These are the former homes of Edna Rae Gillooley, Edna Rae Francemore, Edna Rae, Edna Rae Alexander, Edna McRae Roberts, Erica Dean, Keri Flynn and Ellen McRae—all one person who eventually changed her name for a ninth and final time to Ellen Burstyn. Her name changes were the

3271 and 3277 Hazelwood Street, located south of Joy Road, east of Dexter Avenue.

result of her parents divorcing and remarrying and her taking on various stage names and marrying three spouses herself. Her mother sent her and her brother to St. Mary's Academy in Windsor for a time, and when they returned, Edna attended Hutchens Intermediate School and Cass Tech High School. She endured a troubled, abusive childhood, living at two homes next to each other. Starting in 1940, she lived in the home on the left for about seven years. At the age of fourteen, Edna's mother and her third husband bought the house next door, where they lived another four years or so until Edna turned eighteen, the day she promised herself she'd leave home. She then worked at J.L. Hudson's department store and took a second job at the Patricia Stevens Modeling School, where she spent the next five months saving her money and buying clothes at a discount. She then boarded a Greyhound bus and headed to Dallas, Texas, where she took more modeling gigs, before eventually landing in New York City, where she enrolled at The Actor's Studio (she's been copresident since 2000). It wasn't long before Burstyn was noticed on Broadway and appeared on TV, launching what would become an impressive and admired acting career that included stellar performances in such movies as *The Last Picture Show*, *The Exorcist* and *Alice Doesn't Live Here Anymore*. She is one of the few who has won an Oscar, Emmy and Tony Award.

ART CLOKEY

8230 Fullerton Avenue
GPS Coordinates: 42.38130, -83.15133

You may not know his name, but you certainly know the characters he came up with. Who can forget TV's *Gumby and Pokey* and that old Sunday morning staple *Davey and Goliath*? They were the creation of animator and director Arthur Farrington. That was the name he was born with here in Detroit, but things changed when Art's father died in a car accident when he was nine. Art was living with his father after his parents' divorce, and when his father passed away, he went to California to live with his mother and stepfather. His stepfather shunned him and placed him in a children's home, where he was adopted at the age of twelve by Joseph Clokey. Art's new adoptive father was a well-respected music teacher who filled Art's life with many creative outlets and adventures that would inspire his future

8230 Fullerton Avenue, located west of I-96, northeast of Grand River Avenue. (It no longer exists.)

career. This pioneer in the stop-motion animation and claymation field also provided the voice of Pokey, made commercials for Budweiser and Coke and made the title sequences for the '60s beach movies *How to Stuff a Wild Bikini* and *Dr. Goldfoot and the Bikini Machine*. And if you're wondering why Gumby's head is shaped the way it is, Clokey based it on his biological father's haircut, which was piled up high on the right side of his head. Clokey died in his sleep at the age of eighty-eight in 2010.

FRANCIS FORD COPPOLA

17540 Kentucky Street
GPS Coordinates: 42.42144, -83.15918

This is where the family lived. Not *that* "family" but the Coppola family. The family's patriarch, Carmine, was the flautist, arranger and assistant orchestra director of the *Ford Sunday Evening Hour*, an ongoing radio concert

17540 Kentucky Street, located east of Wyoming Avenue, north of West McNichols Road.

series sponsored by Ford Motor Company. He was also first flautist for the Detroit Symphony Orchestra. But it was his son, Francis Ford Coppola, who would propel the family name to new heights. He was born in 1939 and lived in this home until 1942, when his dad was named principal flautist for the NBC Symphony Orchestra and the family moved to New York. Francis's middle name came from the place he was born, Henry Ford Hospital, as well as his father's employer at the time. Coppola, of course, became an acclaimed director of films like *The Godfather* trilogy, *The Conversation* and *Apocalypse Now*, with his father serving as the composer of several of his films.

ROGER CORMAN

16536 Greenlawn Street
GPS Coordinates: 42.41300, -83.15076

Roger Corman grew up to be the "Pope of Pop Cinema" and "King of the Cult." This is where he grew up until he turned fourteen and his family moved to Beverly Hills, California. He fell in love with the movies there but chose to follow in his engineer father's footsteps at Stanford University. He got a job at U.S. Electrical Motors, and after just four days, he went into his boss's office and said, "I've made a terrible mistake." With his brother in the film business, Roger got a job in the mailroom at 20th Century Fox. During that time, Corman began writing and directing and eventually wanted a bigger stake in the business, so he started his own production company. He could stretch a dollar like no one else, making low-budget, drive-in must-sees with titles like *Monster from the Ocean Floor*, *The Beast with a Million Eyes* and *Attack of the Crab Monsters*. He would often reuse footage, hire the same people and shoot movies in days, like the nonmusical version of *Little Shop of Horrors* (reportedly shot in two days and one night). Whether they worked in one of Corman's schlocky horror films, teen comedies or his version of an Edgar Allan Poe story, many of Hollywood's biggest names started with him, including Jack Nicholson, Francis Ford Coppola, Martin Scorsese and Robert DeNiro. Did switching careers and keeping a tight rein on the purse strings pay off? Corman died at the age of ninety-eight on May 9, 2024, with a net worth of $200 million.

16536 Greenlawn Street, located west of Livernois Avenue, south of West McNichols Road.

PAM DAWBER

8244 Indiana Street
GPS Coordinates: 42.35504, -83.15503

29064 Summerwood Road
GPS Coordinates: 42.51035, -83.34728

The stars of TV's *Mork and Mindy* went to high schools located 6.3 miles from each other on the same street, 13 Mile Road, at the same time. Robin Williams went to Detroit Country Day School and Pam Dawber went to North Farmington High School. Yet their paths would not cross until years later, when they were 2,300 miles from Detroit and cast in the *Happy Days* spinoff. Dawber was born in Detroit and lived on Indiana Street but moved to Farmington Hills around the age of ten to this 1961 home on Summerwood Road. After graduation, she attended Oakland Community College for a short period before she was offered a modeling contract with Wilhelmina Models in New York City. She appeared in TV commercials and Robert

8244 Indiana Street, located south of Joy Road, east of Wyoming Avenue. (It no longer exists.)

29064 Summerwood Road, located south of 13 Mile Road, west of Middlebelt Road.

Altman's *A Wedding* before she was cast as Mindy. To see if the combination of Dawber and Williams would work for the new show, its producers took footage from Williams on *Happy Days* and film of Dawber from a failed sitcom she appeared in and spliced them together. It worked. Dawber went on to win the People's Choice Award for Favorite Female Performer in a New TV Program for this show and her next sitcom, *My Sister Sam*.

ARETHA FRANKLIN

7415 La Salle Boulevard
GPS Coordinates: 42.36293, -83.09859

Woodlawn Cemetery
19975 Woodward Avenue
GPS Coordinates: 42.44304, -83.12772

The "Queen of Soul" lived in several homes in and around Detroit throughout her life. This is one of them, her home between the ages of

7415 La Salle Boulevard, located north of West Grand Boulevard, east of Linwood Street.

Woodlawn Cemetery, 19975 Woodward Avenue, located south of 8 Mile Road. (Lower level of the main mausoleum, section 185–188.)

five and eighteen in the La Salle Gardens area. Aretha's father, Reverend C.L. Franklin, owned the six-thousand-square-foot home until his death in 1984. In 1979, he was shot twice here during what was believed to be an attempted robbery. The incident left him in a coma for five years. The nearby La Salle Park is dedicated to him. In 2013, Aretha sold the home for $81,000, and in May 2023, it was sold for $355,000. Her former bedroom is located above the front porch on the right. From "Respect" to "You Make Me Feel Like a Natural Woman" and "Freeway of Love," Franklin sold over 75 million records, making her one of the world's best-selling music artists. She passed away on August 16, 2018, at the age of seventy-six from pancreatic neuroendocrine cancer.

MARVIN GAYE

19315 Appoline Street
GPS Coordinates: 42.43363, -83.17214

3067 Outer Drive
GPS Coordinates: 42.43496, -83.14509

Imagine who might have been invited to a holiday party at Berry Gordy's house in 1960. Then imagine an unknown guy named Marvin Gay being invited to perform for guests. But so impressed was Gordy that he signed Gaye to his Tamla label, with Gay adding an "e" to his last name to distance himself from his abusive minister father. He released a few singles and did session work and songwriting, but it wasn't until Gaye released "Pride and Joy" in 1963 that his career took off. It became a top 10 hit. After that, the hits kept coming—"How Sweet It Is (To Be Loved by You)," "Ain't That Peculiar" and "I Heard It Through the Grapevine" and duets like "Ain't No Mountain High Enough," "Ain't Nothing Like the Real Thing" and "You're All I Need to Get By," all with Tammi Terrell. With early success came fame, money and a house on Appoline Street. Gaye's later success brought more fame, more money, struggles with cocaine and depression—and a bigger home on Outer Drive. One of Gaye's biggest songs, "What's Goin' On," would follow—but not without a fight with Gordy, who, at first, refused to release the song because he thought it was too political. The song reached number 1 on the R&B charts and sold over two million copies, earning Gaye

19315 Appoline Street, located south of West Outer Drive, west of Wyoming Avenue.

3067 Outer Drive, located west of Livernois Avenue.

a new $1 million contract with Motown Records, the most lucrative deal for a Black recording artist at the time. Gaye was one of the last to leave Detroit when Gordy moved the business to Los Angeles. Number 1 hits followed him there: "Let's Get It On," "I Want You" and "Got to Give It Up." Amid tax problems, an escalating cocaine addiction and a falling-out over the release of an edited, unfinished album, Gaye parted ways with Motown. He signed with CBS records, where he had the biggest success of his career with "Sexual Healing." It spent ten weeks at number 1 and earned Gaye two Grammy Awards. Despite the accolades, Gaye's last year was filled with a relentless schedule of live performances and TV appearances, depression, debt worries and paranoia from cocaine. He finished his tour and moved in with his parents in Los Angeles to recover. On April 1, 1984, a heated argument ensued between Gaye and his father, resulting in Marvin Sr. shooting his son twice. Marvin's final words were, "I got what I wanted….I couldn't do it myself, so I made him do it."

MARLA GIBBS

1100 Atkinson Street
GPS Coordinates: 42.38058, -83.09180

4003 Clements Street
GPS Coordinates: 42.38953, -83.13377

Chicago-born actress/comedienne Marla Gibbs lived in Detroit twice. The first time was after her divorced father died and she was sent here to live with her mother and stepfather at their home on Atkinson Street. She went to Northern High School for one semester but returned to Chicago and lived with her grandmother so she could finish high school where she started. After graduating, she attended business school and landed a job as a receptionist at the Gotham Hotel back in Detroit. The upscale hotel for Black guests at 111 Orchestra Place (between Woodward Avenue and John R Street, north of Mack Avenue) was demolished in 1963. Gibbs lived on Clements Street during her time there and, on the side, "ran the numbers" with her mother. She later left the Gotham Hotel and took a job at United Airlines, which eventually transferred her to Los Angeles. Always interested in acting, Gibbs began taking acting lessons and going to workshops, which

1100 Atkinson Street, located west of the Lodge Freeway, south of Chicago Boulevard. (It no longer exists.)

4003 Clements Street, located west of Dexter Avenue, north of the Davison Freeway. (It no longer exists.)

led her to audition for the role of Florence Johnston, the wise-cracking maid on the hit *All in the Family* spinoff, *The Jeffersons*. She won the role, but not knowing if the gig would last, she continued to work at United Airlines for the first two years of the series. Gibbs was nominated for an Emmy for Outstanding Supporting Actress in a Comedy five times for her role. It also led to Gibbs having a starring role in her own popular comedy, *227*.

BERRY GORDY

2648 West Grand Boulevard
GPS Coordinates: 42.36428, -83.08838

918 West Boston Boulevard
GPS Coordinates: 42.38516, -83.09384

Motown Records founder Berry Gordy owned this sprawling home on West Boston Boulevard until 2002. It was a far cry from the upstairs apartment where he and his family lived prior to that (what is now the Motown Museum). Gordy bought that house in 1959, turning the lower level into a recording studio and offices. He didn't know it then, but this inauspicious

2648 West Grand Boulevard, located west of the Lodge Freeway.

918 West Boston Boulevard, located east of the Lodge Freeway.

start would lead him, in 1967, to buy one of the largest residential homes in the area, what has since become known as the Motown Mansion. The mansion comprises 10,500 square feet, with an adjacent 4,000-square-foot pool house (where Michael Jackson learned to swim) on 2.2 acres. Gordy made extensive updates and renovations over the time he lived in the home. He then moved Motown Records to Los Angeles in 1972.

The mansion has a secret tunnel that leads from the main house to the pool, still lined with portraits of Motown stars. It boasts ten bedrooms, a bar, a bowling alley, a sunroom, a projection room and a ballroom, and at one time, it had a five-hole golf course out back. It was built by lumber baron and real estate mogul Nels Michaelson, who spared no expense. Michaelson bought one thousand acres in this area and subdivided it, putting his grand home front and center. It has had many owners, including those who have continued to preserve and update it. In 2017, one hundred years after the mansion was built, its current owner bought it for $1.65 million.

DAVID ALAN GRIER

2200 West Boston Boulevard
GPS Coordinates: 42.38030, -83.10647

When he lived in this house as a kid, David Alan Grier described himself as being a "Blerd" (a Black nerd). But by the time he made his way through Cass Tech High School, the University of Michigan and then Yale School of Drama, he could have easily described himself as a multifaceted actor and singer. He won acclaim out of the gate in several Broadway productions, including *A Soldier's Play* and *Dreamgirls*, and on the big screen in Robert Altman's *Streamers* and Keenan Ivory Wayans's *I'm Gonna Git You Sucka*. Wayans then cast Grier in his groundbreaking TV variety series *In Living Color*, in which Grier earned himself a new descriptor: comedian. Grier showed his comedic chops in sketch after memorable sketch, like "Men on Film," in

2200 West Boston Boulevard, located east of the Lodge Freeway.

which his character Antoine Merriweather offered movie ratings in the form of "snaps up." He has worked almost nonstop ever since, his familiar face appearing in numerous sitcoms, movies and theatrical productions, adding author, game show host, Tony winner, Grammy nominee, *Saturday Night Live* host, Hollywood Walk of Fame recipient and more to a lengthy list of descriptors that started with Blerd.

BILL HALEY

395 Florence Street
GPS Coordinates: 42.41265, -83.11829

When people talk about the beginning of the Rock and Roll era, most cite the song "Rock Around the Clock" as the starting point. The sound was totally new, unlike the standards of the Frank Sinatras or Bing Crosbys of the time. It came from Bill Haley and His Comets, and though the initial release was lackluster, the rerelease swept like wildfire across the country. And it only picked up more steam when the band appeared on *The Milton Berle Show* and *The Ed Sullivan Show*. When the song was used in the 1955 movie *The Blackboard Jungle*, it became a number 1 hit. The song reached a whole new audience in the 1970s, when it was used as the theme song for the

395 Florence Street, located west of Woodward Avenue, north of the Lodge Freeway. (It no longer exists.)

popular TV series *Happy Days* for its first two seasons. Producers created their own *Happy Days* song for the remainder of the series due to the popularity of *Grease* causing the licensing of '50s songs to skyrocket. Bill Haley lived in the Highland Park area of the city until the age of seven, when the Great Depression forced his family to look for opportunity elsewhere, which they found in Pennsylvania. Haley spent the last few months of his life dealing with the effects of a brain tumor, alcoholism and a crumbling marriage. He died at the age of fifty-five in 1981.

MICHAEL JACKSON'S "GRAVE"

Woodlawn Cemetery
19975 Woodward Avenue
GPS Coordinates: 42.44141, -83.12279

One of the more unusual Detroit celebrity sites is here at Woodlawn Cemetery; it's the gravesite of Michael Jackson. Actually, *he's* not buried here, but tributes marking his passing are. After the "King of Pop" died, the Motown Museum received an overwhelming amount of fan memorabilia on its doorstep, including stuffed animals, gloves, cards, et cetera. What do you do with all that stuff? Well, you bury it. Two side-by-side plots

Woodlawn Cemetery, 19975 Woodward Avenue, located south of 8 Mile Road. Through the entrance, take the first right, and the headstone is located on the right at the roadside.

were donated, a handful of private companies paid for the headstone and vaults, a ceremony was held and, now, under that marker lie two coffins filled with all that stuff.

ALEX KARRAS

16174 Prest Street
GPS Coordinates: 42.41017, -83.19759

This is the home of legendary Detroit Lions defensive tackle Alex Karras. While playing for the home team from 1958 to 1970 (except for 1963, when he was suspended for betting on games), Karras lived here on Prest Street. He was a colorful character on the local Detroit scene, whether he was serving drinks behind the bar of Lindell A.C. (which he was part owner of and where he was a participant in a storied brawl in 1963) or wrestling Dick the Bruiser for eleven minutes in a stunt that earned him $17,000. His acting side hustle turned into a lucrative second career. He memorably appeared as Mongo in *Blazing Saddles* and played James Garner's toady in *Victor/Victoria*. And he played the stepfather of a Black orphan as the star of TV's popular *Webster*, with his wife, actress Susan Clark.

EDDIE KENDRICKS

16531 Baylis Street
GPS Coordinates: 42.41329, -83.12440

"Get Ready," "Standing in the Shadow of Love" and "Just My Imagination" were chart-toppers for The Temptations, with falsetto-voiced (but actually a tenor) Eddie Kendricks as one of the group's lead singers. When Kendricks and his bandmates moved from Cleveland to Detroit to join Motown Records, they went through numerous member and name changes, finally emerging in 1961 as The Temptations. They began by singing in the background for Mary Wells but soon broke out on their own to become one of the most popular male vocal groups of the 1960s. During this time, Kendricks lived on Baylis Street, the street right behind

16174 Prest Street, located east of Greenfield Road, north of Puritan Avenue.

16531 Baylis Street, located south of West McNichols Road, west of Woodward Avenue.

Gladys Knight's former home. Toward the end of the 1960s, Kendrick (he dropped the "s" he added to make his stage name and returned to his birth name) became disillusioned with the psychedelic way the band was going and went solo. In 1971, before he left, he recorded one last song, "Just My Imagination," which became a number 1 hit. In the 1980s, Kendrick had trouble hitting the high notes he normally could and went to see a doctor, who discovered a "pin drop" of cancer on one of his lungs. Kendrick refused chemotherapy for fear of losing his hair. He continued to sing and, in 1991, had surgery to remove his cancerous lung. But the lung cancer, which he attributed to thirty years of smoking, had spread, and eventually took his life when he was fifty-two in 1992.

KEEGAN-MICHAEL KEY

2430 Woodstock Drive
GPS Coordinates: 42.44583, -83.12661

He's seemingly everywhere: the movies (*Wonka*), the small screen (*Schmigadoon!*, *Key & Peele* reruns, hosting *Saturday Night Live*), the stage (*Hamlet*), commercials (T-Mobile) and books (as an author with his wife, Elle, for *The History of Sketch Comedy: A Journey Through the Art and Craft*

2430 Woodstock Drive, located south of 8 Mile Road, west of Woodward Avenue.

of Humor). Even his voice is everywhere: *The Lion King*, *The Super Mario Bros. Movie*, *Bob's Burgers* and his own podcast. But before that, Keegan-Michael Key was here, on Woodstock Drive. Key was born in Southfield and adopted at birth by a couple who were both social workers. He was a student at Shrine High School and then went to the University of Detroit Mercy, where he got a rich theater experience and started his own improv group. He earned a master of fine arts degree in theater at Penn State, and when he returned home to Detroit, he joined Second City, which led him to Second City in Chicago. This is where he met his comedy partner Jordan Peele, whom he'd team up with on *MAD TV*. Eventually, they landed their own show, *Key & Peele*, for which they won two Emmy Awards (and had eighteen nominations) and a Peabody Award. This, of course, led to all the work mentioned previously and so much more for one of the busiest funnymen in the entertainment industry.

GLADYS KNIGHT

16860 La Salle Avenue
GPS Coordinates: 42.41612, -83.12527

The sheer number of talented, well-known people who once lived within a couple of miles of the Detroit Golf Club is amazing. Gladys Knight was one of them. When she moved from Atlanta to Detroit to join the Motown label, she wanted her kids, Kenya and James, to go to Gesu Catholic School, so she bought this nearby home. She lived here from 1966 to 1973, a time when she and The Pips recorded some of their biggest hits: "I Heard It Through the Grapevine," "If I Were Your Woman" and "Neither One of Us." She also lived for a time on Sherborne Road in the more upscale Sherwood Forest neighborhood. Knight left Motown and eventually Detroit for Buddha Records to seek a broader audience. She got it with the second song to come out on that label: "Midnight Train to Georgia." It became a number 1 hit and her signature song. That song also has a Detroit connection to *The Six Million Dollar Man*'s Lee Majors, who was born in Wyandotte. The song's writer, Jim Weatherly, was friends with Majors and his then-girlfriend, Farrah Fawcett, in Los Angeles. Weatherly called Majors one night and Fawcett answered the phone. He asked her what she was doing, and she said she was "taking a

16860 La Salle Avenue, located south of West McNichols Road, west of Woodward Avenue.

midnight plane to Houston." It stuck with the songwriter, and he crafted a storyline around a superstar who didn't get far, which was a nod to Majors, who was a great football player in college but didn't make the majors (no pun intended).

MARTA KRISTEN

18960 Cherrylawn Street
GPS Coordinates: 42.43068, -83.15513

Birgit Annalisa Rusanen spent the first few years of her life in an orphanage in her native Norway. Her German father was killed in World War II, and her mother gave her up when she was just two months old so she wouldn't have to deal with the burden of having parents who were members of the

Third Reich. In 1949, she was adopted by a Detroit couple, Dr. Harold and Bertha Soderquist, who renamed her Martha Annalise Soderquist. Her adoptive father was a professor at Wayne State University, and Martha attended Farmington Elementary School. At the age of fourteen, Martha did summer stock at the Will-O-Way Theatre in Birmingham. In 1959, her father took the family to Los Angeles for a year's sabbatical, and there, Martha got more involved in acting. She liked it so much that she ended up staying in Los Angeles with a guardian when her family returned to Detroit. During that time, she took the stage name Marta Kristen to reflect her Scandinavian roots. She is best known for her role as the eldest daughter, Judy, of the galaxy-travelling Robinson family on the '60s sci-fi TV show *Lost in Space.*

18960 Cherrylawn Street, located south of 7 Mile Road between Livernois Avenue and Wyoming Avenue.

PIPER LAURIE

2708 Tyler Avenue
GPS Coordinates: 42.39120, -83.12293

She was the unstable, religious fanatic mother of Sissy Spacek in the horror classic *Carrie*, Paul Newman's girlfriend in *The Hustler* and the weirdly wonderful Catherine Martell in David Lynch's original *Twin Peaks*. She was born Rosetta Jacobs in a one-room duplex (through the door on the left) on Tyler Avenue. She lived here until she was six, when her parents sent her sister to a Los Angeles, California sanitarium because she was asthmatic. Rosetta was sent there as well to "keep her company," her mother said. As she wrote in her 2011 memoir, *Learning to Live Out Loud*, she hated those years but eventually saw them as beneficial: "My exile had cultivated an imagination that grew like a giant, sheltering flower. It was a lifetime gift." Their mother and father joined them three years later in California and had them both released. Scared to death of public speaking, Rosetta was given elocution lessons, which led to acting jobs and eventually led to her winning a contest in which the top prize was a screen test. With that, she secured an

2708 Tyler Avenue, located south of West Davison Street, east of Dexter Avenue.

agent, who gave her a yellow sheet of paper with a catchier name for her written on it: Piper Laurie. She landed a seven-year contract with Universal Studios (which included a role in one of the *Francis the Talking Mule* movies) the same day Rock Hudson did. She went on to gain critical acclaim in more movies and TV shows, her last role being in Matthew McConaughey's *White Boy Rick*. Laurie passed away at the age of ninety-one on October 14, 2023.

JOE LEWIS

1683 Edison Street
GPS Coordinates: 42.37866, -83.09909

Signs of Joe Lewis can be found throughout Detroit, from *The Fist* monument at the intersection of Woodward and Jefferson Avenues to downtown's Joe Lewis Greenway biking trail and the *Path of Life* sculpture in Riverside Park, which was made of materials from the demolished Joe Lewis Arena. And these monuments stand for good reason: the man was a Detroit institution

1683 Edison Street, located south of Chicago Boulevard, east of Rosa Parks Boulevard.

and national hero after he delivered a knockout punch to Nazism when he beat Germany's boxing champ Max Schmeling in 1938. Born Joseph Lewis Barrow in Alabama, he moved to Detroit in 1924 when he was ten years old after Klu Klux Klan members threatened his family. Here, in Detroit, Joseph's mother made him take violin lessons to keep him away from gangs, but it didn't stop him from getting involved in a different kind of fighting. Legend has it that for his first big boxing match, he signed his name "Joe Lewis" so his mother wouldn't know he was fighting. He won fifty of his fifty-four fights as an amateur boxer and sixty-six of sixty-nine fights as a professional. He held the World Heavyweight Championship title from 1937 to 1949. He lived in this home on Edison Street at some point in his career. The end of his life was not as illustrious, as he faced tax, drug and mental illness problems. When he died in 1981 at the age of sixty-six due to cardiac arrest in Las Vegas, then-president Ronald Reagan waived the burial requirements for Arlington National Cemetery, and Joe was laid to rest there.

TIM MEADOWS

15851 Inverness Street
GPS Coordinates: 42.40878, -83.12291

In this "meadow" stood the home of Tim Meadows, another former *Saturday Night Live* cast member from Detroit. Next to Darrell Hammond and Keenan Thompson, Meadows was with the show the longest, from 1991 to 2000. As a performer and writer, he created spot-on parody impressions of celebrities like O.J. Simpson, Oprah Winfrey and Tiger Woods and memorable original characters like the Ladies Man, who was also the star of his own movie. That character of Leon Phelps was based on men who frequented the Conant Street and East McNichols Road party store Meadows worked at in high school. He has appeared in countless TV and movie comedies over the years, from *The Office* and *The Goldbergs* to *Mean Girls* and *Grown Ups*. Meadows was born and raised in Detroit and attended Mason Elementary School, Farwell Junior High School and Pershing High School. He then went on to study radio and TV broadcasting at Wayne State University before he headed to Chicago to join the famed Second City comedy troupe.

15851 Inverness Street, located west of Woodward Avenue, north of the Lodge Freeway. (It no longer exists.)

S. EPATHA MERKERSON

14966 Stansbury Ave.
GPS Coordinates: 42.39972, -83.18197

If Reba the Mail Lady from *Pee-wee's Playhouse* was to deliver a package to this address, she'd be dropping it off at the childhood home of Sharon Epatha Merkerson, the actress who got her big break playing Reba. Fun fact, her mother worked for the Detroit Post Office as the only woman in the vehicle operations unit. Sharon graduated from nearby Cooley High School in 1970 and earned a bachelor of fine arts degree in theater from Wayne State University in 1976 and a master in fine arts degree from New York University in 1978. She legally changed her first name to "S." and goes by Epatha, the name of an elementary schoolteacher her father had, who was influential in keeping him in school. When Merkerson appeared on TV's popular *Law & Order* in its first season as a grief-stricken mother of a baby who was accidentally shot, producers were so impressed with her performance that

14966 Stansbury Avenue, located south of Fenkell Avenue, west of Schaefer Highway.

she ended up replacing Dann Florek (also a Detroiter) as Lieutenant Anita Van Buren in seasons 4–20, the longest-running, continuous cast member of the series. Van Buren is also the longest-running Black character to appear in a show in television history. In 2015, Epatha took on the role and currently stars as Sharon Goodwin, the head of the Gaffney Chicago Medical Center on TV's *Chicago Med*. The multi-award-winning, often-nominated actress has also had standout roles in film, including in *She's Gotta Have It* and *Lackawanna Blues*, and on Broadway in *The Piano Lesson*.

TED NUGENT

23251 Florence Street
GPS Coordinates: 42.40974, -83.26811

The Motor City Madman, Uncle Ted, Great Gonzo, Sweaty Teddy, Terrible Ted, the Whackmaster. They're all nicknames for hard rocker Ted Nugent. And he's also been called a few other names for his polarizing political and activist views. But whatever you call him, his birth certificate says his official

23251 Florence Avenue, located east of Telegraph Road, south of West McNichols Road.

name is Theodore Anthony Nugent, born here in Redford on December 13, 1948. And whatever you think about him, it's hard to argue that he knows his way around a guitar. "Wango Tango," "Cat Scratch Fever" and "Stranglehold" are proof of his prowess and songwriting ability. So, how did the Nuge get his start? His aunt, who was an airline stewardess, sent a left-behind, unclaimed guitar to this house, and from the moment the nine-year-old picked it up, he immersed himself in lessons and music theory. By the age of thirteen, Nugent had formed his first band, The Lourds, which opened for The Supremes and the Beau Brummels at Cobo Hall.

RAY PARKER JR.

3780 Virginia Park Street
GPS Coordinates: 42.36310, -83.11445

If it looks like we may need to call the Ghostbusters on this place, it could be because it's the home where Ray Parker Jr. grew up. The singer/songwriter for the Oscar-nominated movie theme song lived on the lower

3780 Virginia Park Street, located west of Dexter Avenue, north of West Grand Boulevard.

level of this Virginia Park Street home. "Ghostbusters" was his biggest hit (others include "A Woman Needs Love," "Jack and Jill" and "You Can't Change That"). But before all that, he was a much-in-demand Motown session musician. At the age of thirteen, he played guitar for The Spinners, and at eighteen, he dropped out of Lawrence Tech to join Stevie Wonder's band, sharpening his musical skills and graduating from what he called Wonder University. At the same time, he was also writing for other artists, including Rufus and Chaka Khan, Barry White and Johnny Mathis. He eventually inked his own deal with Arista Records and formed the band Raydio. Recognizing that Parker could also sing and had the looks to attract a young crowd, Arista talked him into going solo, where he enjoyed his greatest successes. By the way, who won the Academy Award for Best Original Song the year "Ghostbusters" was nominated? That would be Stevie Wonder for "I Just Called to Say I Love You" from *The Woman in Red*.

ROSA PARKS

2672 South Deacon Street
GPS Coordinates: 42.26693, -83.15484

3201 Virginia Park Street
GPS Coordinates: 42.36438, -83.10967

9336 Wildemere Street
GPS Coordinates: 42.37326, -83.11576

Riverfront Towers
250 Riverfront Drive
GPS Coordinates: 42.32486, -83.05541

Woodlawn Cemetery
19975 Woodward Avenue
GPS Coordinates: 42.43964, -83.12120

After Rosa Parks refused to give up her seat on a bus in Alabama, she and her husband, Raymond, lost their jobs, received death threats and were harassed to the point where life became unbearable. In 1957, they fled to Detroit to live with Rosa's brother, Sylvester McCauley, at his Deacon Street home. They lived here until 1959 and then moved to the first-floor flat of a home on Virginia Park Street. In 1977, Raymond died, and Rosa lived here by herself until 1988. She then moved to a home on Wildemere Street, until one night in August 1994, an intruder broke in and assaulted and robbed her of fifty-three dollars. A group of prominent Detroiters, including A. Alfred Taubman, Mayor Coleman Young, Representative John Conyers and radio personality Martha Jean "The Queen" Steinberg, stepped up and got her an apartment at the safer Riverfront Towers. A trust was set up, and along with contributions from Little Caesars owner Mike Ilitch and others, she had her rent paid until she died there in 2005 of natural causes at the age of ninety-two. She is interred in a chapel that was named after her at Woodlawn Cemetery.

In the early 2000s, the Deacon Street home fell into disrepair and faced demolition. Parks's niece Rhea McCauley tried to save it for historical purposes, but no one stepped forward until Berlin-based artist Ryan Mendoza heard about it. He had disassembled a Detroit home before and

2672 South Deacon Street, located west of West Jefferson Avenue, north of West Outer Drive.

reassembled it in Berlin, Germany, and that's exactly what he did with the first Detroit home of the mother of civil rights. It was on display there for a time and shipped back to the United States for showings, and as of this writing, it is set up for viewing inside the Royal Palace of Naples in Italy. In 2021, Parks's Virginia Park Street home was placed on the National Register of Historic Places.

Left: 3201 Virginia Park Street, located west of Linwood Street, north of West Grand Boulevard.

Below: 9336 Wildemere Street, located east of Dexter Avenue, south of Chicago Boulevard.

Riverfront Towers, located west of the Renaissance Center off Jefferson Avenue.

Rosa L. Parks Freedom Chapel, Woodlawn Cemetery, 19975 Woodward Avenue, located south of 8 Mile Road. The chapel is located at the southeast corner of the cemetery.

GILDA RADNER

17330 Wildemere Street
GPS Coordinates: 42.41999, -83.13266

Here on Wildemere Street is the home of Gilda Radner, the very first cast member to be hired on *Saturday Night Live*. She grew up in this stately neighborhood and attended the private University Liggett School in Grosse Pointe Woods eighteen miles away. At this house, she was cared for by a nanny, Elizabeth Gillies, whom she called "Dibby." And it was Dibby whom Gilda based her confused *Weekend Update* correspondent character, Emily Litella, on. Her father, Herman, ran the swanky downtown Statler Hotel (now demolished) until it was discovered he had a brain tumor. He was bedridden at the home and unable to communicate. Two years later, Herman lost his battle, and fourteen-year-old Gilda lost her father. After high school, she attended the University of Michigan to study theater but dropped out to follow her boyfriend to Toronto, where she eventually joined The Second City. This was also where *Saturday Night Live*'s Lorne Michaels

17330 Wildemere Street, located north of West McNichols Road, west of Woodward Avenue.

spotted her for his new show. She left the show in 1980 and married Gene Wilder in 1984. She was married to him until she passed away from ovarian cancer in 1989 at the age of forty-two. Her legacy lives on through Gilda's Club, community gathering places that provide social and emotional support for cancer patients and their families.

JOYCE RANDOLPH

6329 Globe Avenue
GPS Coordinates: 42.40674, -83.14122

Joyce Sirola played Thelma "Trixie" Norton, the wife of Ed Norton, the upstairs neighbors and best friends of Ralph and Alice Kramden on the classic TV sitcom *The Honeymooners*. Sirola was born in this apartment building on Globe Avenue on October 21, 1924. When she began to act, Joyce changed her last name to Randolph to sound "more inviting." Evidently, it worked, as she was invited to become part of what's considered

6329 Globe Avenue, located west of Livernois Avenue, north of the Lodge Freeway.

one of the best TV comedies of all time. Originally, the role of Trixie was envisioned to be an ex–burlesque dancer; at first, the directors cast another Detroiter, Elaine Stritch, in the role, and she filmed the first episode. After that, the show's star and creator, Jackie Gleason, retooled the part to be a typical American housewife. Gleason recalled seeing Randolph in a Clorets breath mint commercial, and that's how she got the part. She played Trixie until the show went off the air. In the 1960s, *The Honeymooners* was revived in sketches on Gleason's new variety shows and as specials, but the parts of Alice and Trixie were recast for various logistical and personal reasons.

DAVID RUFFIN

17385 Parkside Street
GPS Coordinates: 42.42067, -83.13210

Woodlawn Cemetery
19975 Woodward Avenue
GPS Coordinates: 42.44015, -83.12280

No other Motown artist had a high–low range like the extraordinary singer who lived in this house. But when David Ruffin joined The Temptations in 1964, his voice was hidden within the ensemble. One of the label's biggest stars took notice. Smokey Robinson specifically wrote "My Girl" to

17385 Parkside Street, located north of West McNichols Road, east of Livernois Avenue.

Woodlawn Cemetery, 19975 Woodward Avenue, located south of 8 Mile Road. The gravestone is located at section 3, lot 243, grave no. 3.

showcase Ruffin's unique vocal range and stylings, and it became the group's first number 1 hit and signature song. From then on, Ruffin was a lead singer with The Temptations, recording hit after hit, like "Ain't Too Proud to Beg," "I Wish It Would Rain" and "Since I Lost My Baby." But all this went to Ruffin's head and up his nose. His cocaine addiction caused him to show up late to rehearsals, miss concerts and insist that, in the same way Diana Ross was positioned to stand out in her group as Diana Ross and the Supremes, he wanted his group to be called David Ruffin and the Temptations. This didn't fly with founding member Otis Williams, and in 1968, he fired Ruffin. A successful solo career followed, with hits like "What Becomes of the Brokenhearted," "My Whole World Ended" and "Common Man," but so did Ruffin's escalating cocaine addiction. It culminated in his overdose death at the age of fifty in Philadelphia on June 1, 1991.

SOUPY SALES

19373 Renfrew Road
GPS Coordinates: 42.43500, -83.13420

Television was good to Soupy Sales here in Detroit. It got him this home in the exclusive Sherwood Forest area, and it put his comedy on a national stage. Soupy Hines arrived in the Motor City in 1953 from Ohio with a deal for a children's program on WXYZ-TV called *12 O'Clock Comics*. Born Milton Supman, when he became a young disc jockey, he used a variation of his childhood nickname, "Soup Bone," and changed his last name to Hines. But when he signed on to his Detroit TV show, the general manager feared his last name would be confused with the station's sponsor, Heinz, so he suggested Soupy adopt comic Chic Sale's last name. Soupy's show, which also changed its name to *Lunch with Soupy* and, later, *The Soupy Sales Show*, was a long-running hit, and in 1955, it was a summer replacement for the

19373 Renfrew Road, located north of 7 Mile Road, east of Livernois Avenue.

popular national kiddie show *Kukla, Fran and Ollie*. Soupy created memorable characters to play off of, like White Fang, Black Tooth and Pookie, and at some point in the show, he would always take a signature pie to the face. He estimated he was hit with a pie over twenty-five thousand times in his career. Sales added a nighttime show to his arsenal, and in 1961, he brought his show to the ABC station in Hollywood. He also appeared in movies and on game shows and received a star on the Walk of Fame. Sales died in 2009 in New York from cancer at the age of eighty-three.

GEORGE C. SCOTT

18981 Pennington Drive
GPS Coordinates: 42.43103, -83.14855

Great Scott, it's George C.'s house! Yep, this is the boyhood home of Academy Award refuser George C. Scott. He won Best Actor for 1970's *Patton* but passed on it because he felt each nominated performance was individual and couldn't be compared to one another. His mother died in this home when he was eight of blood poisoning, and he was raised by his father, the CEO

18981 Pennington Drive, located north of 7 Mile Road, west of Livernois Avenue.

of Ex-Cell-O Corporation, a now-dissolved aircraft parts and machine tools manufacturer. In high school, he was an usher at the Redford Theatre. After graduating from Redford High School in 1945, he joined the U.S. Marines and then attended the University of Missouri, where he enrolled in journalism but switched to drama after he acted in a play. As he said, "It just clicked, just like tumblers in a safe." He returned to Michigan to make the Jimmy Stewart drama *Anatomy of a Murder* in the Upper Peninsula and then again with his wife, actress Colleen Dewhurst (they married, divorced and then remarried), to start the Theatre of Michigan Co. Its intent was to develop stage plays here and bring them to Broadway, but the first two productions were flops, and the company dissolved a year later. He went on to acclaimed work in *Dr. Strangelove*, *The Hospital* and *The Hustler* and had Broadway hits like *Death of a Salesman* and *Inherit the Wind*. Scott died at the age of seventy-one in 1999 of a ruptured aortic aneurysm.

TOM SKERRITT

12003 Cheyenne Street
GPS Coordinates: 42.37577, -83.17477

Film fans know him from movies like *Alien*, *A River Runs Through It* and *Top Gun*. And TV fans know him from *Picket Fences* (for which he won an Emmy) and *Cheers* (he played Evan Drake, Rebecca Howe's boss). Eagle-eyed film

12003 Cheyenne Street, located north of Plymouth Road, east of Schaefer Highway.

fans of the cult classic *Harold and Maude* will spot him as a motorcycle cop in the film. He filled the role as a last-minute favor for his mentor, director Hal Ashby, after the actor who was playing the cop got thrown off the bike and broke his leg. Skerritt stepped in and is credited as "M. Borrmann." Why that name? Skerritt said he was just looking to help out Ashby, so he said he wanted to be funny and use the name of Hitler's second-in-command, a guy who went missing without a trace. This Cheyenne Street house is Skerritt's boyhood home, where he was the youngest of four children. He went to MacKenzie High School, Henry Ford College and Wayne State University. After that, he transferred from Wayne State University to UCLA, where he became a screenwriter and director. He never had the intention of becoming an actor, but things successfully didn't quite work out the way he planned.

LEVI STUBBS

18512 Santa Barbara Drive
GPS Coordinates: 42.42796, -83.14891

17330 Fairway Drive
GPS Coordinates: 42.41973, -83.13060

Woodlawn Cemetery
19975 Woodward Avenue
GPS Coordinates: 42.44040, -83.12238

Cousin to Jackie Wilson, Levi Stubbs was the lead vocalist of the Four Tops, the popular R&B group known for such enduring hits as "Baby I Need Your Loving," "I Can't Help Myself (Sugar Pie, Honey Bunch)," "Reach Out I'll Be There," "Ain't No Woman Like the One I Got," "Bernadette" and so many more. Yet when the standout baritone was offered top billing of the proposed Levi Stubbs and the Four Tops, he refused it or any solo offers, as the four men were such a tight group. In fact, the original members, including Abdul "Duke" Fakir, Renaldo "Obie" Benson and Lawrence Payton, performed together from 1953 to 1997, until Payton died. One of the only times Stubbs did step away from the act was to do the memorable voice of Audrey II, the carnivorous plant in the 1986 musical film *Little Shop*

18512 Santa Barbara Drive, located south of 7 Mile Road, west of Livernois Avenue.

17330 Fairway Drive, located west of Woodward Avenue, north of West McNichols Road.

Woodlawn Cemetery, 19975 Woodward Avenue, located south of 8 Mile Road. The gravestone is located right off the parking lot, behind the main office.

of Horrors. He made Santa Barbara Drive his home until he moved over to Fairway Drive, which backs up to the Detroit Golf Club. Stubbs suffered a stroke and left the group in 2000; he died in his sleep in 2008 at the age of seventy-two.

THE SUPREMES

Brewster Projects
I-75 and Mack Avenue
GPS Coordinates: 42.35174, -83.04895

Ross
3762 Buena Vista Street
GPS Coordinates: 42.38764, -83.13072

Ballard
3767 Buena Vista Street
GPS Coordinates: 42.38719, -83.13048

Wilson
4099 Buena Vista Street
GPS Coordinates: 42.38605, -83.13368

Last Home of Ballard
17701 Shaftsbury Avenue
GPS Coordinates: 42.42201, -83.23086

Ballard Gravesite
Detroit Memorial Park Cemetery
4280 East 13 Mile Road
GPS Coordinates: 42.51932, -83.06488

Most know The Supremes all lived in the Brewster Projects (now demolished) when they joined Motown Records. But when they started to make it big, Diana Ross, Mary Wilson and Florence Ballard all lived somewhere else together—they all, unknowingly, moved onto the same street. While the group was on tour, a representative from Motown went out to scout places for them to buy. Photographs of homes were shown to them separately, and each picked out a house, only to discover that they all bought homes within a two-block stretch of each other on Buena Vista Street. Ross lived almost directly across the street from Ballard, and Wilson lived in a duplex one block west of them, renting the other side to Cholly Atkins, the famed Motown choreographer. The women's catfighting and jockeying for position is storied (and escalated after Berry Gordy made Ross the lead singer and changed their name to Diana Ross and the Supremes) and led to Ballard's 1967 exit after she turned to alcohol for solace and began showing up drunk and missing performances. Ballard embarked on a less-than-successful solo career with a shady talent agency and endured an abusive marriage that drove her deeper into alcoholism, depression and poverty. She eventually checked herself into rehab at Henry Ford Hospital, and she emerged with newfound sobriety and an interest in singing again. But she would not see a next act. At the age of thirty-two, this singer died at Mt. Carmel Mercy Hospital after suffering cardiac arrest due to a blood clot in one of her coronary arteries. When she departed the act,

The former site of the Brewster Projects, at the corner of I-75 and Mack Avenue.

The Ross home, 3762 Buena Vista Street, located south of West Davison Freeway, west of Dexter Avenue.

The Ballard home, 3767 Buena Vista Street, located south of West Davison Freeway, west of Dexter Avenue.

The Wilson home, 4099 Buena Vista Street, located south of West Davison Freeway, west of Dexter Avenue.

The last home of Ballard, 17701 Shaftsbury Avenue, west of Southfield Freeway, south of 7 Mile Road.

Detroit Memorial Park Cemetery, 4280 East 13 Mile Road, located east of Ryan Road. Proceed through the entrance, and the Eternal Love Mausoleum is straight ahead and to the left. Directly to the right in the north area of section D is the gravestone.

Ballard was replaced by Cindy Birdsong. Ross departed in 1970. Wilson went on with a version of The Supremes until she went solo in 1977. Wilson and Ross appeared together again at the Motown 25 reunion, with much reported backstage drama. And there was an ill-fated attempt at a reunion tour in 2000, but a deeper wedge was forged between the two when Ross demanded $15 to $20 million, and Wilson was offered only $2 to $3 million. With their relationship never repaired, Wilson died in 2021 of hypertensive atherosclerotic cardiovascular disease at the age of seventy-six.

LILY TOMLIN

8917 Byron Street
GPS Coordinates: 42.37720, -83.09263

File this under "Famous comediennes who lived in Detroit-area apartments that were torn down and are now empty fields." Joining a certain iconic TV redhead from Wyandotte is Lily Tomlin, whose family lived in

8917 Byron Street, located west of the Lodge Freeway, south of Chicago Boulevard. (It no longer exists.)

an apartment once located here on Byron Street. She went to nearby Hutchins Intermediate School, Cass Tech (where she was voted "Most Popular" and "Most School Spirited") and Wayne State University. She entered college to study biology but switched to theater when she landed a role in a play. This changed the trajectory of her life, and after doing successful stand-up comedy in town, she moved to New York City. Her big break came when she replaced the departing Judy Carne on *Rowan & Martin's Laugh-In*, which was half-hosted by former Detroiter Dick Martin. She was an instant hit, creating such memorable characters as Ernestine, the telephone operator; five-and-a-half-year-old Edith Ann; and Mrs. Judith Beasley, a housewife who dispenses consumer advice. Her movies (*9 to 5*, *Nashville*), Broadway shows (*The Search for Signs of Intelligent Life in the Universe*), stand-up albums (*This Is a Recording*) and more TV shows (*Grace & Frankie*) earned her numerous acting nominations and awards, culminating in a Kennedy Center Honor in 2014 and a Career Achievement Peabody Award in 2022. Giving back to her hometown of Detroit and her college alma mater, she established the Lily Tomlin Endowed Scholarship Fund in 1990 at Wayne State University.

COURTNEY B. VANCE

15096 Appoline Street
GPS Coordinates: 42.40161, -83.17019

The home at 4710 West Grand Boulevard no longer exists, but that's where accomplished actor Courtney B. Vance remembers tanks rolling past his house during the 1967 Detroit riots. Not long afterward, the family moved north to Appoline Street, where a camp counselor at the Boys and Girls Club told Courtney about an available scholarship to the private college prep school Detroit Country Day. Vance applied and got it, and though his parents couldn't afford the rest of what it would take to send him there, they made it work. At Detroit Country Day, Vance immersed himself in school and athletics, playing football and basketball, running track, serving as student council president and joining every club he could. He called it his second home, sometimes spending sixteen-hour days there and riding his bike twenty-five miles to football camp during the summers. It prepared him to go not just to Harvard but also to Yale, where he met his wife, actress

15096 Appoline Street, located south of Fenkell Avenue, west of Meyers Road.

Angela Bassett. He had no intention of pursuing acting, but after his aunt saw him in a play at Harvard, she recommended he should do this as a career, and that's all it took. The Emmy- and Tony-winning actor has starred in hits like *The Preacher's Wife*, *Fences*, *The People vs. O.J. Simpson* and *The Hunt for Red October*.

ROBERT WAGNER

17410 Fairway Drive
GPS Coordinates: 42.42082, -83.13069

So, if Gilda Radner jumped over her back fence, crossed the street and jumped over that neighbor's fence, do you know whose house she would see? Actor Robert Wagner's. He played Number 2 in two *Austin Powers* movies and was the star of the TV hits *It Takes a Thief* and *Hart to Hart*. He was married four times, twice to actress Natalie Wood. Their first marriage lasted from 1957 to 1962, and the second lasted from 1972 until Wood's

17410 Fairway Drive, located south of 7 Mile Road, west of Woodward Avenue.

mysterious, still-unexplained drowning death that occurred in 1981 during a sailing trip to Santa Catalina Island with Wagner and actor Christopher Walken. Wagner was the son of a traveling salesman at Ford, and he lived in this stately mansion that backed up to the Detroit Golf Course from his birth to the age of seven. In 1937, the Wagners moved to the affluent Bel Air area of Los Angeles, where their son Robert caught the acting bug.

DINAH WASHINGTON

4002 Buena Vista Street
GPS Coordinates: 42.38698, -83.13236

The Supremes were not the only legendary singers who lived on Buena Vista Street. Two years before they moved in, Dinah Washington slept here. She lived between the houses where Florence Ballard and Mary Wells would live on Diana Ross's side of the street—but not for long. The

4002 Buena Vista Street, located south of West Davison Freeway, west of Dexter Avenue.

troubled jazz, blues and R&B great with a crystal-clear voice lived here with her sixth husband, Detroit Lions cornerback Dick "Night Train" Lane. Just five months after they were married, they went to bed on December 14, 1963, and Lane awoke to find her dead. Autopsy reports said she died of a lethal combination of amobarbital and secobarbital. She was thirty-nine years old at the time of her death, which was ruled an accident.

JACKIE WILSON

16522 La Salle Avenue
GPS Coordinates: 42.41320, -83.12510

The man known as "Mr. Entertainment" lived here. Singer Jackie Wilson earned and lived up to that title for his electrifying showmanship and fashion style. There's no doubt that his love for boxing influenced his onstage fancy footwork and flips. His life off stage was a different story. Growing up in

16522 La Salle Avenue, located west of Woodward Avenue, south of West McNichols Road.

Highland Park, he had a troubled childhood that included gangs, alcohol and him fathering a child at the age of seventeen. But his love for singing endured, and eventually, he became a lead singer for The Dominoes. After three years, he struck out on his own while also writing songs, and that's when he soared with hits like "Lonely Teardrops," "(Your Love Keeps Lifting Me) Higher and Higher" and "Baby Workout." But his carousing, womanizing, financial and legal issues, survival of a shooting and overcoming the death of two children all took their toll on him in the form of a massive heart attack he had in 1975 while performing on *Dick Clark's Good Ol' Rock and Roll Revue*. While singing "My heart is crying" from "Lonely Teardrops," Wilson collapsed. He was in and out of a coma and was incapacitated for the rest of his life. He died of pneumonia in 1984 at the age of forty-nine.

STEVIE WONDER

3347 Breckenridge Street
GPS Coordinates: 42.34285, -83.09726

18074 Greenlawn Street
GPS Coordinates: 42.42374, -83.15122

When the Judkins moved from Saginaw to Detroit, they lived in apartment 2701 in the Brewster Projects. Calvin and Lula Mae had three children, one of whom was blind. Born six weeks prematurely, their son received oxygen in his incubator that stopped the growth of his eyes and caused his retinas to detach. Enduring an abusive marriage, Lula Mae was determined to get herself and her children out of the situation, so she secretly saved up $8,000 and, when the time was right, left her husband. She moved her family to a home on Breckenridge Street (which no longer stands). By the age of nine, her blind son, Stevland, had learned how to play the piano, drums and harmonica, and he was so good that by the age of eleven, Berry Gordy Jr. had signed him to Motown's Tamla label. People were so astounded by his talent that he was called "Stevie, the Little Wonder." Motown Records producer Clarence Paul flipped it around and came up with his first stage name, "Little Stevie Wonder." But Gordy Jr. did not like one of his artists living on less-than-desirable Breckenridge Street, so he bought the family a home for $18,000 on Greenlawn Street. It was here that Wonder spent

3347 Breckenridge Street, located west of I-96, south of I-94. (It no longer exists.)

18074 Greenlawn Street, located south of 7 Mile Road, west of Livernois Avenue.

his formative years, singing, songwriting and laying the groundwork for a career that has seen 30 U.S. Top 10 Hits, 10 number 1 hits, sales of over 100 million records, 25 Grammy Awards (the most of any solo artist), an Oscar, his induction into the Rock and Roll Hall of Fame and a Kennedy Center Honor, to name a few accomplishments. While he has not lived in the Greenlawn Street house for decades, Wonder still owns the property.

7

NORTHEAST DETROIT

SONNY BONO

5380 Holcomb Avenue
GPS Coordinates: 42.38378, -83.00457

On the east side of Detroit is a modest little home where half of the mega-popular '60s and '70s Sonny & Cher singing duo began his groovy life. This was the boyhood home of Salvatore "Sonny" Bono. He was born in 1935

5380 Holcomb Street, located east of Van Dyke Avenue, south of Gratiot Avenue.

and lived here until 1942, when his father, a truck driver, headed west and moved the family to California. There, Sonny broke into the music business, and he eventually met a homeless runaway named Cher Sarkisian, who wanted to be a performer. They teamed up and reached superstardom with hits like "The Beat Goes On" and "I Got You Babe," and even landed their own popular TV variety show. The pair divorced in 1975, and Sonny eventually traded entertainment for politics when he was elected to the U.S. House of Representatives. Sonny died in 1998 at the age of sixty-two as a result of injuries he sustained in a skiing accident at Heavenly Ski Resort in Lake Tahoe.

EMINEM

19946 Dresden Street
GPS Coordinates: 42.44311, -82.99986

If you want to see prolific rapper Eminem's childhood home today, you'll have to look at the cover of 2000's *The Marshall Mathers LP*. A fire destroyed the house in 2013, and it was later leveled. At the time, Eminem sold off seven hundred bricks from the house that sat below 8 Mile Road, with proceeds going to the Marshall Mathers Foundation, an organization dedicated to

19946 Dresden Street, located south of 8 Mile Road, east of Hoover Street. (It no longer exists.)

helping disadvantaged and at-risk Detroit youth. The $300-plus bricks sold out. Eminem was born Marshall Bruce Mathers III in 1972. At the age of seventeen, when he became seriously interested in rapping, he changed his name to M&M (for Marshall Mathers). To avoid legal issues with the candy company, he adopted the phonetic spelling that he goes by today. He also goes by the nickname "Slim Shady," which was used in the title of his second album in 1999, *The Slim Shady LP*.

JESSE OWENS

18561 Binder Street
GPS Coordinates: 42.42971, -83.06425

In 1936, track and field star Jesse Owens won four gold medals at the Olympics, which were held in Berlin, Germany, at the time of Hitler's rise to power. On the first day of competition, Hitler offered congratulatory handshakes to his German athletes but no one else. The International Olympic Committee insisted that he shake hands with all the winners or none at all. The dictator picked the latter. Owens's triumphs foiled Hitler's

18561 Binder Street, located south of 7 Mile Road, east of Conant Street.

hope for German domination at the games, and he was welcomed back to the United States with a ticker tape parade in New York City. Despite his popularity, he still experienced racism and discrimination and was reduced to taking various menial jobs—that is, until a friend and former competitor from Detroit offered him a job in the personnel department at Ford Motor Company. Owens and his family moved to Detroit and lived in this house on Binder Street from 1942 to 1946, when he served as the liaison between Black and white workers at Ford and as an advocate for Black rights. Owens then left for Chicago, where he opened his own public relations firm. He fell on hard times and held various jobs until Dwight Eisenhower named him a goodwill ambassador in 1955, and he began getting endorsement deals and paid speaking engagements for major companies like Quaker Oats, Johnson & Johnson and Ford. In 1976, he was awarded the Presidential Medal of Freedom. A six-pack-a-day smoker, Owens died from lung cancer at the age of sixty-six in 1980.

TOM SELLECK

10530 Lakepointe Street
GPS Coordinates: 42.41540, -82.95567

10530 Lakepointe Street, located south of Vernier Road, north of I-94.

This may be the perfect house for Tom Selleck to show up at to try to peddle the reverse mortgages he hawked on TV. That's because he lived here until the age of three. In 1949, his carpenter father moved the family to California, where he found success in real estate. This is also where young Tom grew up to become the star of *Magnum P.I.* and—almost—*Indiana Jones*. Selleck was cast in *Raiders of the Lost Ark*, but CBS told him he couldn't do both

Indiana Jones and *Magnum P.I.*, so he had to pull out three weeks before *Raiders* was to start filming. As it turned out, a TV actors strike followed, and he actually could have done the movie, but Harrison Ford had already been named as his replacement. In the popular TV series *Magnum P.I.*, Thomas Magnum always wore a Detroit Tigers baseball cap as a nod to Selleck's birthplace, which was also made the birthplace of his character.

TOM SIZEMORE

11937 Hamburg Street
GPS Coordinates: 42.43300, -82.99718

Actor Tom Sizemore and his family lived here on Hamburg Street in the upper flat of his grandparents' house. He was born in 1961 and lived here until 1974, when the Sizemores moved to Shelby Township. While he lived here, he went to Wilkins Elementary School and then Von Steuben Middle School. Later, he went to Bishop Gallagher and then graduated from Wayne

11937 Hamburg Street, located west of Gratiot Avenue, southeast of East McNichols Road.

State University with a bachelor of fine arts degree in theater. He also earned a master's degree from Temple University. After a promising start in Hollywood that included such hit films as *Born on the Fourth of July*, *Saving Private Ryan*, *Heat*, *Natural Born Killers* and more, his life spiraled out of control with drugs, domestic violence issues, stints in and out of jail and rehab, a sex tape and more. But he continued to work through it all, with more movies and TV shows (including reality shows related to his drug issues), and he even fronted a band. On February 18, 2023, he suffered a brain aneurysm that he didn't recover from. Doctors informed his family that there was nothing they could do and that they needed to make an end-of-life decision. Sizemore passed away on March 3, 2023, at the age of sixty-one.

8
DETROIT SUBURBS

ANN ARBOR

VIRGINIA PATTON MOSS

2205 Melrose Road
GPS Coordinates: 42.26660, -83.71483

Ann Arbor is no Bedford Falls, but this is where you'll find the former home of Virginia Patton Moss. And though you may not recognize her name, she herself said, "I've been in more homes than Santa Claus." That's because she played George Bailey's brother's wife, Ruth, in the holiday classic *It's a Wonderful Life*. And for her, it was a wonderful life. She ditched the movies in 1949 after marrying her husband, Cruse Moss, and moved to Ann Arbor for most of the rest of her life. She was active at the University of Michigan and was the president of the Patton Corporation on State Street, a corporate real estate investment firm. She also had the distinction of being General George S. Patton's niece. After her husband died in 2018, she moved to Albany, Georgia, to be close to her son. This last living adult cast member of *It's a Wonderful Life* died at the age of ninety-seven on August 18, 2022.

2205 Melrose Street, located west of I-23, north of Washtenaw Avenue.

BERKLEY

CURTIS ARMSTRONG

1658 Wiltshire Boulevard
GPS Coordinates: 42.49932, -83.17312

Curtis Armstrong says that not a day goes by that people don't recognize him as Booger, the character he played in the *Revenge of the Nerds* movies. And there's no telling how many utter his line from his very first movie, *Risky Business*: "Sometimes, you just have to say, WTF." Curtis Armstrong was also memorable on TV's *Moonlighting* and in Savage Steve Holland's *Better Off Dead*. After he was born at Detroit's Harper Hospital in 1953, his family moved to Switzerland for a few years, and then in 1967, they moved back and lived at this home in Berkley. He graduated from Berkley High School in 1972 and then attended Western Michigan University before he transferred to Oakland University's Academy of Dramatic Art program. Armstrong graduated from Oakland University in 1975, and in 2023, the man who specializes in underdogs and outcasts, like Dudley "Booger" Dawson from Adams College, was welcomed back to Oakland, where he received an honorary doctorate of arts degree.

MARSHALL CRENSHAW

2727 Oakshire Avenue
GPS Coordinates: 42.49719, -83.19593

The basement of the Crenshaw house in Berkley served as a home base for after-school practice sessions of a band called Astigafa. The name was an acronym for "a splendid time is guaranteed for all," a lyric from The Beatles' "Being for the Benefit of Mr. Kite" from their *Sgt. Pepper* album. Marshall Crenshaw was the band's self-appointed lead guitarist. He had picked up the instrument at the age of ten and was raised by a music-loving father who took his kids to Jimi Hendrix Experience, Cream and MC5 concerts. He graduated from Berkley High School in 1971. Crenshaw's big break came when he auditioned and made the cut to appear as John Lennon in Broadway's *Beatlemania*. Songwriting and his smash-hit first album featuring "Someday, Someway" followed. Along with a slew of other hits, he also played Buddy Holly in *La Bamba*, had a bit part in fellow-Detroiter Francis Ford Coppola's *Peggy Sue Got Married*, served as a New York City radio host and, in 2017, appeared with The Smithereens as a guest vocalist following the death of the band's lead vocalist and his friend, Pat DiNizio.

1658 Wiltshire Boulevard, located west of Woodward Avenue, south of 12 Mile Road.

2727 Oakshire Avenue, located south of 12 Mile Road, east of Greenfield Road.

BIRMINGHAM/WEST BLOOMFIELD

TIM ALLEN

1085 Suffield Avenue
GPS Coordinates: 42.55494, -83.23310

Tim Allen was born in Denver, Colorado, but made his way to Detroit through tragic circumstances. When he was eleven, his father, while driving home from a football game, was killed by a drunk driver. When he was thirteen, his mom married her high school sweetheart from Michigan, and the family moved to Birmingham. This was a *Brady Bunch* house before there was a *Brady Bunch*, with Allen and his five siblings moving into his stepdad's house along with his three children. Allen graduated from Seaholm High School in 1971 and then initially attended Central Michigan University before he transferred to Western Michigan University. Throughout these years, Allen struggled with alcohol and sold dope, culminating in his arrest at the age of twenty-five for trying to smuggle a pound and a half of cocaine through a Michigan airport. He served over two years in jail, but he came out on the other side of all this to achieve great fame. He pursued stand-up comedy, and his "he-man" stand-up routine was the inspiration for his mega-hit sitcom *Home Improvement*. The TV comedy ran from 1991 to 1999 and was set in Detroit (look for Motor City cues around Tim Taylor's house, like the Detroit Lions pennant next to the fireplace and his wife's Detroit Opera House coffee mug). After that, Allen reached mega-star status with the popular *Santa Clause* movies and as the voice of *Toy Story*'s Buzz Lightyear. He also had a second hit sitcom, *Last Man Standing*.

DICK BEALS

139 East Brown Street
GPS Coordinates: 42.54402, -83.21470

There's a piece of art next to a parking structure in Birmingham where a very interesting guy lived. His house is no longer standing, but "X" marks the spot at the intersection of Pierce and Brown Streets, where Dick Beals

1085 Suffield Avenue, located west of Woodward Avenue, south of Quarton Road.

139 East Brown Street, located west of Woodward Avenue, south of East Maple Road.

grew up. But he actually grew up in a different way; due to a glandular problem, he never went through puberty. He stood at just four feet, seven inches tall and weighed just seventy pounds. But this led to a life well lived as a one-of-a-kind, ever-youthful voiceover actor in Hollywood. His career started at the age of eight, when he and his mother, as they were coming out of the downtown Detroit Hudson's department store, ran into her old classmate who worked at the Jam Handy Organization, an industrial film company. The classmate initially thought Beals was about four years old, and the man recognized the appeal of working with someone older who sounded and appeared younger, as they could take direction well. This led to Beals getting acting gigs and radio work at a young age before he attended Michigan State University, where he became a member of the cheerleading squad and majored in radio broadcasting and puppetry. He eventually landed a role on the popular *Green Hornet* radio show, which got him voiceover jobs in Los Angeles. His career included him portraying characters with all the major animation studios, but he is perhaps most famous for giving a voice to Davey on fellow Detroiter Art Clokey's *Davey and Goliath* and Speedy Alka-Seltzer in hundreds of commercials from 1954 to 1964. As a testament to Beals's talent, when directors were casting for the animated *Addams Family* TV series, Beals beat out over three hundred boys who tried out for the role of adolescent N.J. Normanmeyer—at the age of sixty-five. He passed away in 2012 at the age of eighty-five at Vista Gardens Memory Care in Vista, California.

JIMMY HOFFA

Hoffa Home
1614 Ray Court
GPS Coordinates: 42.77233, -83.27703

Airport Service Lines
7 South Perry Street
GPS Coordinates: 42.63626, -83.29045

Machus Red Fox
6676 Telegraph Road
GPS Coordinates: 42.54255, -83.28560

Damman Hardware
6650 Telegraph Road
GPS Coordinates: 42.54237, -83.28532

White Chapel Cemetery
621 West Long Lake Road
GPS Coordinates: 42.58401, -83.16350

The end of Martin Scorsese's *The Irishman* shows Al Pacino (as Jimmy Hoffa) sitting on a deck at a lake house. That's a movie location, but this house on Ray Court is the real deal. This is where Hoffa left around 1:15 p.m. on July 30, 1975, for a 2:00 p.m. lunch meeting at Machus Red Fox (now Andiamo's) with reputed mobsters "Tony Jack" Giacalone and "Tony Pro" Provenzano. He made one stop on the way down to Airport Service Lines in Pontiac to see his unofficial and checkered past secretary Louis "The Pope" Linteau, but he wasn't in. Around 2:15 p.m., Hoffa called his

1614 Ray Court, located north of Clarkston Road, east of Joslyn Road.

1614 Ray Court, Square Lake side, located north of Clarkston Road, east of Joslyn Road.

The former location of Airport Service Lines, 7 South Perry Street at Pike Street, located west of North Woodward Avenue, south of M-59.

The former Machus Red Fox (now Andiamo), 6676 Telegraph Road at Maple Road.

The former Damman Hardware (now Planet Fitness), Bloomfield Plaza, 6650 Telegraph Road at Maple Road.

Left: The former Damman Hardware (now Planet Fitness), located at the south corner wall of Bloomfield Plaza, 6650 Telegraph Road at Maple Road.

Below: White Chapel Cemetery, 621 West Long Lake Road, Temple of Memories mausoleum at the south end of the cemetery. (Second floor to the left of the front door, section D, in the back.)

wife, Josephine, to say that he had been stood up. He made the call from a pay phone outside Damman Hardware (now Planet Fitness) in Bloomfield Plaza, behind the restaurant. While this is hard to verify, the original brick wall out front has drilled holes in it that could have been where the pay phone was. Witnesses have said they saw Hoffa pacing back and forth next to his 1974 green Pontiac Grand Ville on the north side of the restaurant during this time. He went back to the pay phone just before 3:30 p.m. and made one other call to Linteau to see if he knew where Provenzano and Giacalone were. Linteau said he didn't know where they were. That was the last anyone heard from Hoffa. And while we don't know where Jimmy was buried, we do know where his wife of thirty-seven years was laid to rest. Josephine died at the age of sixty-two in 1980 of small stroke syndrome and was buried at White Chapel Cemetery. Her husband was legally declared dead in 1982.

ELMORE LEONARD

2192 Yarmouth Road
GPS Coordinates: 42.55539, -83.24230

Chances are that some, part or all of each book that Elmore Leonard wrote from the 1980s until his death in 2013 was written here. We're talking *Glitz*, *Freaky Deaky*, *Killshot*, *Get Shorty*, *Rum Punch*, *Cuba Libre*, *Be Cool*, *Out of Sight*, *Tishomingo Blues* and many more. The acclaimed novelist wrote

2192 Yarmouth Road, located east of North Cranbrook Road, south of Quarton Road.

four to five pages a day in longhand on custom-made, sixty-three-page unlined yellow pads. When he completed a page or two, he'd type it out on his typewriter to see how it looked. He never used a computer because he said it sounded too dull, like it's not doing anything for you. Leonard moved from New Orleans to Detroit when he was nine and graduated from the University of Detroit Jesuit High School in 1943. He spent three years in the navy, where he earned the nickname "Dutch" after Detroit Tigers pitcher Dutch Leonard. When his tour of duty ended, he attended the University of Detroit, where he graduated in 1950 with a degree in English and philosophy. While he was entering writing contests, submitting articles to magazines and writing short stories on the side, he got a job as a copywriter on the Chevrolet account at Campbell-Ewald Advertising, which he held until the career he was destined to have took hold. Known for his rich character development and dialogue, Leonard said one of his most important rules in writing was to "try to leave out the part that readers tend to skip."

SAM RAIMI

25050 Devon Lane
GPS Coordinates: 42.51837, -83.2916

The Birmingham kid who used his dad's Super 8 camera to make short horror films with his friends at Wylie E. Groves High School graduated to writer and/or director of the Tobey McGuire *Spider-Man* films, *A Simple Plan*, the *Darkman* franchise and, of course, *Evil Dead*. It was the latter film from this Michigan State Spartan that first caught the attention of Hollywood. Raimi and his longtime actor friend Bruce Campbell and producer Robert Tapert hit up family, friends and private investors to raise funds to make *Evil Dead*. They shot most of the film in Morristown, Tennessee, for weather reasons, but when principal filming finished, they came back to Michigan for some additional shooting and even shot scenes here at Raimi's house. Raimi grew up in the Birmingham area (technically, this home is in Franklin Village), the son of the late Celia (who owned Lulu's Lingerie shops) and Leonard (who owned home furnishings and appliance stores). Of particular interest is this home's garage, where Raimi filmed part of *Evil Dead*'s cabin cellar scenes. It also housed the Oldsmobile Delta

25050 Devon Lane, located north of 13 Mile Road, west of Telegraph Road.

88 that Leonard bought new in 1973. This vehicle has made a cameo in one form or another in almost every movie Raimi has directed. Raimi has five children and is married to Gillian Greene, which also makes him the son-in-law of the late actor Lorne Greene of TV's *Bonanza* and *Battlestar Galactica* fame.

DAVID SPADE

6407 Buxton Court
GPS Coordinates: 42.54465, -83.35544

Look up *snark* or *smartass* in the dictionary, and if comedian David Spade's picture isn't there, it should be. He has carved out a comic career playing that kind of guy, from his stand-up to his time on *Saturday Night Live* in the '90s and even to his movie career, which has included starring in such hits as *Tommy Boy* and *Black Sheep* and voicing the character of Emperor Kuzco in *The Emperor's New Groove*. Post–*Saturday Night Live*, Spade also had a hit TV

6407 Buxton Court, located north of West Maple Road, east of Orchard Lake Road.

show, *Just Shoot Me!*, which ran from 1997 to 2003. His teaming with buddy Chris Farley on both *Saturday Night Live* and in the movies was comedy gold. But this would play out for only a short time, as Farley died of an overdose in 1997. Spade was born in 1964 and lived in this home until he was four years old, when his family moved to Scottsdale, Arizona.

NOEL P. STOOKEY

288 West Lincoln Street
GPS Coordinates: 42.53926, -83.21670

In 1950, twelve-year-old Noel P. Stookey moved from Maryland to this house in downtown Birmingham. He graduated from Seaholm High School, where he was part of a doo-wop group called The Birds of Paradise. He fine-tuned his musical talent at Michigan State University but dropped out in his junior year when his family moved to Pennsylvania. He eventually found his way to New York City as an entertainer, catching the attention of a club manager who asked if he'd like to join a folk trio. Had Stookey said no, there would be no Peter, Paul & Mary—Paul being Noel, who used his middle

288 West Lincoln Street, located west of Woodward Avenue, south of Maple Road.

name for the group. They became one of the most popular folk groups of all time, recording hits like "If I Had a Hammer," "Puff, the Magic Dragon," "Leavin' on a Jet Plane" and "500 Miles." Noel also performed as a solo artist, composing the nuptials standard "Wedding Song (There Is Love)." Peter, Paul & Mary officially broke up in 2009, following the death of Mary Travers from leukemia.

ELAINE STRITCH

18210 Birchcrest Drive
GPS Coordinates: 42.42495, -83.13665

280 Harmon Street
GPS Coordinates: 42.55094, -83.21834

Emmy- and Tony-winning actress Elaine Stritch grew up at 18210 Birchcrest Drive. She once asked her father how she was supposed to remember a long address like that, to which he answered, "A girl's of age when she's eighteen. A guy's of age when he's twenty-one. And what does it amount

18210 Birchcrest Drive, located south of 7 Mile Road, west of Woodward Avenue.

280 Harmon Street, located west of Old Woodward Avenue, across from Booth Park.

to? Not a goddamn thing. 18-21-0." After graduating from Sacred Heart Academy, Stritch moved to New York City to break into acting. She became a Broadway fixture, starring in such shows as *Company*, *A Little Night Music* and her one-woman show, *Elaine Stritch at Liberty* (she made "I'm Still Here" and "The Ladies Who Lunch" her signature songs). TV audiences will recognize her as Alex Baldwin's irascible mom on *30 Rock* but won't recognize her as Dorothy Zbornak from *The Golden Girls* because, she admitted, "I blew the audition." The role instead went to Bea Arthur. Stritch was married to actor John Bay (of Bays English Muffins) until his death in 1982. She was the Carlyle Hotel's grand dame resident until she moved back to Detroit toward the end of her life to be closer to her family. She moved to Harmon Street in 2013, trading a room at the Carlyle for a $1.5 million condo at the Dakota in Birmingham, across from Booth Park. She soon regretted it. In typical Stritch crankiness, she said, "I don't have a damned thing to do except take walks in Birmingham. I'm about as unhappy as anybody can be." She died the following year in her sleep at the age of eighty-nine; she had previously been diagnosed with stomach cancer and was living with diabetes.

ROBIN WILLIAMS

Intersection of Woodward Avenue and Opdyke Road
GPS Coordinates: 42.58690, -83.24738

Robin Williams was a long way from Ork when he lived here at Stoneycroft. That was the name of the Williams family's forty-room mansion (with Robin occupying the entire third floor), which stood on seventy-two acres surrounded by a stone wall. Prior to being owned by the Williams family, the home was owned by Theodore McManus, who ran McManus, John and Adams, one of the largest advertising agencies in the United States. The agency's headquarters were located right across the street from the property (a big commute for someone who had the Cadillac automobile account). McManus was a prominent Roman Catholic and built the St. Hugo Church on part of his property in honor of his boys, Hugo and Hubert, who died young. He also built the Stoneycroft Hills Golf Course on his property but never played it. After the deaths of McManus and his wife, Stoneycroft was owned and rented by various families, including the Williamses. Robin went to Detroit Country Day from 1964 to 1968, and

The former property of Stoneycroft Estate, located at the corner of Woodward Avenue and Opdyke Road.

his father worked for Lincoln-Mercury. When his father retired, the family moved to California. In 1980, the mansion burned down, and the property was sold and developed as the Stoneridge Office Complex. The picture here shows the estate's original stone wall that still stands along Woodward Avenue, which the home faced.

CLARKSTON

VALERIE BERTINELLI

4910 Clarkston Road
GPS Coordinates: 42.75767, -83.35145

Because of her father's job at General Motors, Valerie Bertinelli and her family moved around the country often, so much so that she describes

4910 Clarkston Road, located east of Sashabaw Road.

herself as a "GM brat." In 1968, Andy Bertinelli was transferred to GM's Pontiac plant, and the family lived in this home near Pine Knob Music Theater until 1971. Little did young Valerie know that years later, she would marry one of the world's greatest guitarists, Eddie Van Halen, and that he'd be rocking that music venue that was just a few minutes down the street. While she lived here, Valerie was a student at Bailey Lake Elementary School and Clarkston Middle School. From Michigan, her father was transferred again, this time to California, where Valerie became interested in acting. At the age of twelve, she landed a JCPenney commercial. After seeing Valerie in an episode of the short-lived show *Apple's Way*, Norman Lear cast her as Barbara Cooper, the youngest daughter on the hit series *One Day at a Time*. Since then, she's had another hit sitcom, *Hot in Cleveland*, and become a best-selling author and star of her own Food Network cooking show, *Valerie's Home Cooking*.

DEARBORN

CHAD EVERETT

6006 Middlesex Street
GPS Coordinates: 42.33336, -83.18091

If it weren't for his agent changing his name, Raymon Lee Cramton would have been the star of the popular '70s TV drama *Medical Center*. But he was more than happy to change his name to Chad Everett because he was tired of telling people how to spell his real name: "Raymond, no 'd,' and Crampton, no 'p.'" Everett was born in Indiana but grew up in Dearborn, where he attended Fordson High School and then Wayne State University, graduating in 1960 with a degree in mass communications. Aside from his role as Dr. Joe Gannon on *Medical Center*, he was a frequent guest on countless other TV shows, from *The Man from U.N.C.L.E.* to *Murder, She Wrote* and *The Nanny*. He also appeared in movies, including *The Singing Nun*, *Mulholland Drive* and *Airplane II*. Everett died in 2012 from lung cancer at the age of seventy-five, a year after his wife of forty-five years, actress Shelby Grant, died of a brain aneurysm.

FERNDALE

ALICE COOPER

3022 Goodrich Street
GPS Coordinates: 42.47166, -83.12429

1250 Brown Road
GPS Coordinates: 42.70599, -83.27433

On Goodrich Street in Ferndale sits the early boyhood home of Vincent Damon Furnier. His family lived here and in East Detroit until Vincent was twelve. They then moved to Arizona after Vincent had a series of illnesses that caused them to seek a better climate. In high school, Vincent formed a band

6006 Middlesex Street, located north of Ford Road, east of Greenfield Road.

3022 Goodrich Street, located west of Hilton Road, south of I-696.

with friends that they called the Earwigs. They performed at local gigs, went through several name changes and eventually moved to Los Angeles. During this time, Vincent drew inspiration for his band from the films *Whatever Happened to Baby Jane* and *Barbarella*, incorporating makeup and women's clothing, throwing live chickens into the audience, et cetera. When it was brought to their attention that their current band's name, Nazz, was already taken by Todd Rundgren's band, Vincent searched for a name that would be the total opposite of what the audience saw on stage. So, they took the name of a character from a wholesome TV show: Alice Cooper, the housekeeper from *Mayberry R.F.D.* As Alice Cooper, the band caught the eye of another outsider, Frank Zappa, who signed them to a three-album deal. But with slow sales of their first two albums and a feeling that Los Angeles just "didn't get it," Vincent moved his band back to his hometown of Detroit, where he hoped those more accustomed to the Stooges and MC5 would "get them." We did. The band took up residence at a farm on Brown Road in Auburn Hills. The farm, with the barn they practiced in, is long gone, replaced by ABB Robotics. Out at the road was the apron of the driveway that led to the property until a road resurfacing project bulldozed it in June 2024. The move to Detroit paid off for Vincent and the band. Alice Cooper was on fire with successful albums and tours for a couple of years. But as fast as they rose to fame, they eventually ran their course and broke up. That, however, was not the end for Vincent. With built-in credit to the name, Vincent legally changed

1250 Brown Road, now ABB Robotics, where the farm's driveway remained at the roadside until a road widening project bulldozed it in June 2024, located east of Joslyn Road, north of I-75.

his name in 1975 to Alice Cooper and mounted a wildly successful solo music (and acting) career that continues to draw fans. His legacy as the "Godfather of Shock Rock" will no doubt endure, as there's hardly a student alive who doesn't end the year singing "School's Out."

GROSSE ILE

MAX GAIL

7825 Bellevue Road
GPS Coordinates: 42.12300, -83.14352

When they reworked the unsold pilot of *The Life and Times of Captain Barney Miller* in 1975, the character of Kazinski (played by *Hill Street Blues*'s Charles Haid) was changed to Detective Stan Wojciehowicz and was recast with Max Gail in the role. Other characters changed as well, along with the title, and this version of *Barney Miller* ran from 1975 to 1982. The director of the show couldn't pronounce "Wojciehowicz," so he shortened it to "Wojo," which worked itself into the dialogue of the characters of New York City's Twelfth Precinct. Gail was born and raised in this house on Bellevue Road,

7825 Bellevue Road on Grosse Ile.

half of one of the two sets of twins born to Maxwell and Mary Gail of Grosse Ile. His sister Emily (from the other set of twins) is the well-known Detroit booster who started the grassroots Say Nice Things About Detroit campaign dating to the '70s and '80s. Max went to Grosse Ile High School and got an MBA from the University of Michigan. After college and before he headed to California to pursue acting, Gail was an instructor at the University Liggett School in Grosse Pointe Woods.

THE GROSSE POINTES

ANITA BAKER

2 Dodge Place
GPS Coordinates: 42.38456, -82.90009

Behind these gates, right on the shores of Lake St. Clair, sits the 7,300-square-foot home that R&B/soul songstress Anita Baker once lived in. Built in 1987 on the location where the Horace Dodge and Rose Terrace Mansions once stood, the estate was bought by Baker in 1993, following her seven Grammy Award wins from her hit songs, "Rapture," "Sweet Love," "Ain't No Need to Worry," "Giving You the Best That I Got" and "Compositions." At some point, she packed up and left but still owned the property. In November 2023, the home went up for sale for $1.8 million. The listing had no interior pictures and said the home had been vacant for years and likely needed significant repairs: "new owners can choose to restore the home or start fresh with a new one on the lot." As of this writing, the home has still not sold.

JULIE HARRIS

15410 Windmill Pointe
GPS Coordinates: 42.36452, -82.92472

In 1923, investment banker William P. Harris commissioned famed New York architect Alfred Hopkins to build an estate on Lake St. Clair in Grosse Pointe. As his privileged family grew, which included a middle daughter, Julie,

2 Dodge Place, located off Jefferson Avenue, north of Cadieux Road.

15410 Windmill Pointe, located southeast of Jefferson Avenue, northeast of Alter Road.

he brought in Detroit architect Hugh Tallman Keyes to double the home's size to 9,500 square feet. Julie grew up here and went to University Liggett School, but she did not become the society debutante her mother wished her to be. She became something much more. Her mother lived long enough to see her become, at the time, the only actress to win five Tony Awards (Audra McDonald has since won six). And she saw her daughter win an Academy Award for Best Actress for her first film role in *The Member of the Wedding*. Other great film roles followed, including starring opposite James Dean in his first film, *East of Eden*; she also starred with Paul Newman in *Harper* and Marlon Brando in *Reflections in a Golden Eye*. For television, she received eleven Emmy nominations (winning three), including for her role as Lilimae Clements on the popular '80s primetime soap *Knots Landing*. And not to be left out of the Grammys, her mantel also has one of these awards for Best Spoken Word Recording for *The Belle of Amherst*. Toward the end of her illustrious career, Harris earned a National Medal of the Arts, a Kennedy Center Honor and another Tony for Lifetime Achievement. In 2013, Julie Harris passed away from congestive heart failure at the age of eighty-seven.

JOHN HUGHES

743 Rivard Boulevard
GPS Coordinates: 42.39690, -82.91345

John Hughes wrote "Vacation '58" as a short story for *National Lampoon* magazine in 1979. This became the basis for the wildly popular *National Lampoon's Vacation* movie and the *Vacation* sequels. In the short story, readers are along for the ride with the Griswold family, who lived at 74 Rivard Boulevard in Grosse Pointe, Michigan. Griswold paid homage to the downtown Detroit street of the same name. But there is no 74 Rivard Boulevard in Grosse Pointe. However, if you add a 3 to the end of the address and make it 743 Rivard, you'll be at the boyhood home of John Hughes himself. His family lived there until he was about twelve, before they moved to Chicago, where most of his films are set. The prolific comedy writer/director went on to create such monster hits as *Home Alone*; *Ferris Bueller's Day Off*; *The Breakfast Club*; *Sixteen Candles*; *Planes, Trains and Automobiles*; *Pretty in Pink*; and so many more. Unexpectedly, he died in 2009 of a heart attack at the age of fifty-nine while taking a walk in Manhattan.

743 Rivard Boulevard, located east of Mack Avenue, north of Charlevoix Street.

JACK KEROUAC

1407 Somerset Street
GPS Coordinates: 42.38716, -82.93991

Hotel Savarin
13115 East Jefferson Avenue
GPS Coordinates: 42.37111, -82.95125

On August 14, 1944, Jack Kerouac and his girlfriend Edie Parker were awakened in their New York City apartment by a friend, Lucien Carr, who told Kerouac he had just murdered a man who'd made homosexual advances toward him. Shortly thereafter, Carr was arrested, and Kerouac was thrown in jail as a material witness. (Depending on the source, Kerouac

1407 Somerset Street, located south of Mack Avenue, northeast of Chalmers Street.

13115 East Jefferson Avenue, located northeast of Conner Street.

either failed to report the crime or helped dispose of the killer's Boy Scout knife.) To get released, Jack needed to post $500 bail, which he didn't have, and his father refused to pay. Edie didn't have it either, but her Grosse Pointe family did. However, her mother, Charlotte, told her that the only way they'd pay was if Jack and Edie made their relationship legitimate. So, they got married while Kerouac was still in jail, and he got the cash to get sprung. To pay it back, Jack said they'd move to Detroit, where he'd find a job. They lived in Charlotte's home on Somerset Street (her parents had divorced) and he got a job at Fruehauf Trailer Company and Federal Mogul. After growing restless in his pedestrian surroundings, Jack walked down the street to the Rustic Cabins Bar on Kercheval Avenue and lamented that "there was no tragedy in Grosse Pointe." Yearning for his own kind, Kerouac returned to New York City, and Edie followed a short time later. It was at this time that Kerouac began doing drugs, and Benzedrine got the best of their marriage. Edie returned to Detroit and had their marriage annulled in 1946. In the years that followed, Kerouac still had affection for Edie, and on his cross-country road trips, he would attempt to see her. A baseball fan, he liked to stay at the Hotel Savarin, as he found that's where several of the Detroit Tigers roomed. The famed Beat novelist died in 1969 at the age of forty-seven from an abdominal hemorrhage caused by his heavy drinking. Edie died in Grosse Pointe in 1993 at the age of seventy-one from heart disease and diabetes.

J.K. SIMMONS

1617 Roslyn Road
GPS Coordinates: 42.44732, -82.90053

People in this neighborhood see Simmons daily. In fact, it's probably safe to say that most of us see J.K. Simmons daily. He's the actor who plays Professor Nathaniel Burke in the Farmers Insurance commercials. He also voiced the yellow M&M in the candy company's commercials from 1996 to 2013. And then there's his Academy Award for Best Supporting Actor for his intense portrayal of band director Terence Fletcher in *Whiplash.* He also played J. Jonah Jameson in fellow Detroiter Sam Raimi's *Spider-Man* films. J.K.'s father was a music teacher at Parcells Middle School in Grosse Pointe when the family lived here. Young Jonathan Kimble Simmons was a student

1617 Roslyn Road, located east of Greater Mack Avenue, north of Vernier Road.

at Ferry Elementary School until 1965, when the Simmons family moved to Worthington, Ohio. When Simmons broke into professional acting, there were already several variations of "Jonathan Simmons" registered with various actors' unions. But "J.K." was available, so he grabbed it for himself.

HARRISON TOWNSHIP

DEAN CAIN

Selfridge Air National Guard Base
44875 North Jefferson Avenue
GPS Coordinates: 42.61800, -82.83687

Perhaps the most famous person with the shortest stay in Detroit was Dean Cain. He was born Dean George Tanaka on July 30, 1966, the son of Roger and Sharon Tanaka. His father, an army serviceman, and his mother divorced before he was born. Shortly after Dean's birth, Sharon moved to Los Angeles with him and his older brother. When Dean was three, Sharon married writer/director Christopher Cain, and Cain adopted both brothers. Dean, of course, grew up to be an actor (this was after he signed with the Buffalo Bills as a free agent but blew out his knee, ending that career path). His most notable role was as Clark Kent/Superman opposite Teri Hatcher in TV's *Lois & Clark: The New Adventures of Superman*, which ran from 1993 to 1997.

Selfridge Air National Guard Base, 44875 North Jefferson Avenue, located off M-59, east of I-94.

HIGHLAND

DAX SHEPARD

2377 North Milford Road
GPS Coordinates: 42.66244, -83.61920

Dax Shepard was born in rural Highland, where he lived in Highland Green Estates until around his first birthday. His parents divorced when he was three, and he moved around the area several times—not always in the best family situations. He went to Muir Junior High School in Milford and graduated from Walled Lake Central High School in 1993. Little did he know that his future wife, actress Kristen Bell, whom he would meet in Hollywood, lived just around the corner in Huntington Woods, about twenty miles away at the time. Dax was named by his mom after a character in the Harold Robbins book *The Adventurers*. The book depicts the life of Diogenes Alejandro Xenos (Dax, for short), an international playboy who has experienced the best and worst of life. Shepard graduated magna cum laude from UCLA with a degree in anthropology, and a few years later, he joined the Los Angeles improv group The Groundlings. His big break came when Ashton Kutcher cast him in his candid camera–style show *Punk'd*. He

2377 North Milford Road, located north of M-59, south of Middle Road.

went on to appear in TV's *Parenthood* and *The Ranch* and was the writer/director/star of the films *Brothers Justice* and *Hit and Run.* Shepard also hosts the popular podcast *Armchair Expert.*

HOWELL

MELISSA GILBERT AND TIMOTHY BUSFIELD

313 West Washington Street
GPS Coordinates: 42.60651, -83.93370

It's not exactly the *Little House on the Prairie*—more like the 2,500-square-foot house on West Washington Street in Howell. This is where TV's *Little House* actress Melissa Gilbert and actor/director Timothy Busfield (*thirtysomething, The West Wing*) lived after they were married in 2013. Gilbert met Busfield in a bar in Los Angeles, and the two immediately hit it off. But there was a hitch if the relationship was to go anywhere. Busfield said that if the two were to get married, Gilbert would have to move to his home state of Michigan (he was born in Lansing). She said yes to both. The couple settled in Howell and

313 West Washington Street, located south of Grand River Avenue, west of North Michigan Avenue.

lived there until 2018, when work demands in New York City became too much to handle through a commute and they relocated to the Big Apple.

HUNTINGTON WOODS

KRISTEN BELL

8366 Huntington Road
GPS Coordinates: 42.47999, -83.15927

13155 Hart Avenue
GPS Coordinates: 42.48433, -83.18025

10864 Lincoln Drive
GPS Coordinates: 42.48260, -83.17301

Huntington Woods was home to actress Kristen Bell—actually, "homes" to Kristen Bell, as she lived in three of them here. After her parents divorced when she was a toddler and her mother divorced a second time, Bell was split between two of the three nearby homes at a time. Bell went to Burton Elementary School and Norup Middle School and graduated in 1998 from Shrine Catholic High School, where her senior class voted her "Best Looking Girl." She did community theater at Stagecrafters in Royal Oak and had an uncredited role in the locally filmed movie *Polish Wedding*. And in her junior year at Shrine, she starred as Dorothy in *The Wizard of Oz*. This all prepared her for a New York move, going to college at New York University's Tisch School of the Arts. Bell went on to star in TV's *Veronica Mars* and *The Good Place*, as well as in the films *Forgetting Sarah Marshall* and Disney's mega-hit *Frozen* franchise as the voice of Princess Anna. In 2013, she married fellow Detroiter Dax Shepard.

Opposite, top: 8366 Huntington Road, located west of Woodward Avenue, facing the Detroit Zoo's lion exhibit.

Opposite, middle: 13155 Hart Avenue, located west of Woodward Avenue, south of 11 Mile Road.

Opposite, bottom: 10864 Lincoln Drive, located west of Woodward Avenue, south of 11 Mile Road.

INKSTER

MALCOLM X

4336 Williams Street
GPS Coordinates: 42.27765, -83.31293

Malcolm X was born Malcolm Little on May 19, 1925, in Omaha, Nebraska. At the age of twenty, he went to prison for burglary, and while he was there, some of his family, who then lived in Detroit, converted to Islam. They told Malcolm that if he, too, converted, they would help him get out of prison. When he was paroled, he joined his family members in Detroit, as well as the Nation of Islam. It was when he lived here, in this house on Williams Street, that he changed his name to Malcolm X and became the face of the Nation of Islam. It was common for those in the religion to change their last name to an X, choosing to drop their birthname because they were often names that had been given to their families by enslavers. Malcolm would change his name once again on his Muslim-required trip to Mecca, which also changed his life. During his pilgrimage, he converted to Sunni Islam, a more mainstream branch of the religion, and became el-Hajj Malik el-Shabazz.

4336 Williams Street, located north of I-94, west of Inkster Road.

El-hajj indicates a person has completed their trip to Mecca, and *Malik el-Shabazz* indicates a person has converted to Sunni Islam. In 1965, at the age of thirty-nine, the once-extremist, controversial leader was assassinated by three Nation of Islam members. His Michigan home is listed in the National Register of Historic Places and is, as of this writing, undergoing renovations to become a museum.

MONROE

CHRISTIE BRINKLEY

711 East Ninth Street
GPS Coordinates: 41.90490, -83.39550

Christie Brinkley went from this house to become a household name when she appeared on three consecutive *Sports Illustrated* swimsuit issue covers, from 1979 to 1981. She was born Christie Lee Hudson on February 2, 1954, the daughter of Herbert and Marjorie of Monroe. The Hudson family moved to Canoga Park, California, when Christie was young, but her parents divorced

711 East Ninth Street, located west of I-75, east of Telegraph Road, south of River Raisin.

soon thereafter. Marjorie then married TV writer/producer Donald Brinkley (*Medical Center*; *Trapper John, MD*), who adopted Christie. After college, she moved to Paris to study art, and there, she was discovered by photographer Errol Sawyer at a local post office. Brinkley spent twenty-five years as spokesmodel for CoverGirl, appeared on over five hundred magazine covers, married and divorced Billy Joel, had an iconic cameo in *National Lampoon's Vacation* and survived a 1994 helicopter crash in Colorado.

VALERIE HARPER

610 West Elm Avenue
GPS Coordinates: 41.92508, -83.40164

Sisters, Servants of the Immaculate Heart of Mary in Monroe describes itself as "Catholic women drawn together in community and bound together by faith." It's hardly a place where you'd expect to find Mary Tyler Moore's future Jewish neighbor, Rhoda Morgenstern. But in 1949, when actress Valerie Harper (who was actually Catholic) was ten years old, she and her sister were boarded here at what was then St. Mary's Academy.

610 West Elm Avenue, located west of I-75, east of Telegraph Road, north of River Raisin.

Their brother went to the neighboring Hall of the Divine Child. Harper's father was a lighting salesman and moved the family around the country every two years. The Harpers put their children in boarding schools like this so they could focus on their studies without being bothered by the patriarch's frequently erratic schedule. But in 1951, in the era of the atom bomb and with hysteria over it sweeping the nation, Harper's father moved the family to the less-populated, less-of-an-atom-bomb-target town of Ashland, Oregon.

REDFORD TOWNSHIP

RICHARD KIEL

19782 Negounee
GPS Coordinates: 42.43457, -83.31265

As an adult, Kiel certainly would not have fit through the front door of the Detroit home he was born in. Actor Richard Kiel grew to be seven feet, two inches tall due to acromegaly, a condition linked to gigantism from

19782 Negounee Street, located south of West Grand River Avenue, east of Inkster Road.

a pituitary gland problem that overproduces growth hormones. This is where Kiel lived until his family moved to California when he was nine. He played Jaws, the villainous henchman in two James Bond films, *The Spy Who Loved Me* and *Moonraker*. To take the part, he turned down the role of Chewbacca in *Star Wars* because he thought he could bring more to the Bond role. Jaws was originally supposed to die at the end of *The Spy Who Loved Me*, but test audiences loved him, so they rewrote the end and brought his character back for *Moonraker*. There was talk of having him come back in *For Your Eyes Only*, but a change in the key players who made the film nixed his third appearance. He was also cast as the title character in TV's *The Incredible Hulk*, but after he began shooting the pilot, producers didn't think he was bulky enough, so they parted ways and reshot with Lou Ferrigno. Kiel also had memorable roles in *Silver Streak* and *Happy Gilmore*, and in one of his first roles, he can be seen walking out of the gym in Jerry Lewis's *The Nutty Professor*. Kiel died of coronary artery disease in 2014 at age seventy-four.

ROCHESTER

MADONNA

2036 Oklahoma Avenue
GPS Coordinates: 42.68757, -83.17370

In 2001, when the Ciccone family put their Rochester home up for sale, a father and son came up with a plan to buy it and then resell it on eBay. They did this because this wasn't just any home—this was Madonna's childhood home. They bought the home for $270,000 and then developed a marketing plan to sell it. They set up a thirty-day auction on eBay, scheduling it to end on September 20, 2001. It got international attention, and eventually the bids reached $999 million. This was in the early days of eBay, and the online auctioneer had never seen anything like it. But at that price, the executives knew something must be wrong. Who would pay that kind of money for a 2,700-square-foot home in Rochester, Michigan? As an investigation began to unfold, 9/11 happened, and everyone withdrew their bids, leaving the home unsold. In November 2001, a private auction

2036 Oklahoma Avenue, located north of Walton Boulevard, east of Brewster Road.

house in Toledo contacted the father and son and offered to auction the home off—the deal being if the home didn't sell, the auction house would buy it for its appraised value. Thinking it had a potential gold mine on its hands, the auction house sent "plants" to show up on auction day, and of course, one of the "plants" won the bid. For whatever reason, the auction house let it sit for three years, and the home went into disrepair. They ended up selling it at a loss for $91,700. In 2008, the home was sold again and experienced a suspicious fire. In 2012, it was sold again for about $90,000, and after renovations, it was most recently sold for almost $500,000. This home, which backs up to the fourth hole of Brookwood Golf Club, is where the Material Girl lived between the ages of twelve and eighteen. She graduated from nearby Rochester Adams High School in 1976.

JONI MITCHELL

King's Cove Condominiums
GPS Coordinates: 42.69732, -83.14695

Verona Apartments
92 West Ferry Avenue
GPS Coordinates: 42.36112, -83.06894

In 1965, Canadian-born folk singer Joni Anderson was performing at Penny Farthing in Toronto when she met Chuck Mitchell, a fellow folk singer from Rochester, Michigan. He was immediately attracted to her and convinced her that they could team up and find steady work at coffeehouses in the United States. They packed up and moved to Rochester, where, two months later, the pair were married in the backyard of his parents' home, formerly located where the tennis courts now stand at Kings Cove, a condominium complex

Above: King's Cove, located on the north side of West Tienken Road, between Livernois Avenue and North Rochester Road.

Opposite, top: King's Cove, located on the north side of West Tienken Road, between Livernois Avenue and North Rochester Road. The second left leads to the tennis courts. (The home no longer exists.)

Opposite, bottom: 92 West Ferry Avenue, located east of Cass Avenue, west of Woodward Avenue.

off of Tienken Road. As Chuck and Joni Mitchell, the couple moved to downtown Detroit to a fifth-floor walk-up in the Verona Apartments. While playing at area coffeehouses, Joni began experimenting with alternative guitar tunings and composition. Attention began to turn to her, with Joni making frequent appearances on the CBC show *Let's Sing Out*. After less than two years of marriage, the couple divorced. Joni Mitchell would, of course, reach superstardom as a solo artist, with such hits as "Both Sides Now" and "Big Yellow Taxi." And she accumulated numerous awards, from a Kennedy Center Honor to a number 50 spot on the *Rolling Stone* list of the 200 Greatest Singers of All Time.

BOB SEGER

The Farm
GPS Coordinates: 42.69402, -83.17490

In Rochester Hills, between Brewster Road and Livernois Avenue, south of Tienken Road, stood a 120-acre cattle farm that was owned by a couple of developers who, in 1970, weren't ready to develop it. Instead, they rented out the house and barn to some young musicians for $300 a month. From the fall of 1970 to the summer of 1974, this was the place where Bob Seger and his bandmates would jam. It was a remote enough area that their neighbors wouldn't complain about the loud late-night music (although one in particular recalls hearing them). Prior to this, the band had been playing at the home next to the parents of Seger's manager, Ed "Punch" Andrews. They lived on Pine Lake and could no longer tolerate the noise. The farm became a sort of compound, with many bandmates taking up residence there, though part of the rental agreement said no one was supposed to live there. Seger himself lived in Waterford. As Bob Seger and the Silver Bullet Band began coming into its own, the band no longer needed the farm. And by 1976, the developers had turned it into the Brookwood Golf Club and subdivision, which still stands. The home was where the tennis courts are now located. As noted in Madonna's home entry, she lived at the edge of this property, on what is now the fourth hole of the golf course. She has said in interviews that she could hear music in the distance coming from the farm. This means, at one time, Bob Seger and Madonna could have been considered next-door neighbors of sorts before either made it big.

Brookwood Golf Club, located on West Tienken Road, between Brewster Road and Livernois Avenue. (The barn no longer exists.)

ROMEO

KID ROCK

70100 Henry Ross Drive
GPS Coordinates: 42.80882, -83.08612

Growing up, Robert James Ritchie lived among picturesque apple orchards and horse stalls in a 5,600-square-foot home on 5.5 pastoral acres in Romeo. It's not exactly what you'd picture for the rap rock/country rock redneck-y musician who would become megastar Kid Rock, but his hardworking "Daddy Rock" owned the Crest Lincoln-Mercury car dealership in Sterling Heights. A self-taught musician, Ritchie was a student at Romeo High and released his first studio album at the age of seventeen. The origin of his name? Richie would hear from club owners and audience members that they liked to hear "that white kid rock." A big proponent of Detroit, he has won American Music and People's Choice Awards, wed and divorced Pamela Anderson and performed at the Super Bowl. He also owns his own recording label and clothing line, has survived political firestorms and, believe it or not, is an ordained minister.

70100 Henry Ross Drive, located north of 32 Mile Road, east of Dequindre Road.

ROYAL OAK

DR. JACK KEVORKIAN

333 East 11 Mile Road
GPS Coordinates: 42.49062, -83.14058

223 South Main Street
GPS Coordinates: 42.48845, -83.14384

White Chapel Cemetery
621 West Long Lake Road
GPS Coordinates: 42.59109, -83.16426

There was no assisted suicide involved in the demise of Dr. Jack Kevorkian. "Dr. Death" died at William Beaumont Hospital in 2011 at the age of eighty-three from a blood clot lodged in his heart, and he was buried at White Chapel Cemetery. He claimed to have assisted in 130 deaths by suicide of ailing and

333 East 11 Mile Road, located east of Main Street.

Above: 223 South Main Street, located south of 11 Mile Road.

Left: White Chapel Memorial Cemetery, 621 West Long Lake Road, section H, grave no. 6178. The grave is located to the right of the entrance, toward Crooks Road.

terminally ill people. During much of this time, he lived above what was then Mr. B's, a longtime neighborhood bar, and at Avenue Eleven Apartments, both in Royal Oak. In 1990, Kevorkian began his assisted suicide run by fabricating a Thanatron (Greek for "instrument of death") using forty-five dollars' worth of materials that allowed the sick to deliver a lethal cocktail to themselves. The machine was often used in the back of Kevorkian's van or a motel room, sometimes followed by Kevorkian dropping the body off at a nearby hospital. After the death of his first "patient," who had Alzheimer's disease, Kevorkian was charged with first-degree murder. But the case was later dismissed. Kevorkian beat prosecutors four times, until a segment on a CBS News program showed him administering life-ending drugs to a man with Lou Gehrig's disease. Kevorkian spent eight years in jail, and as far as anyone can tell, he never aided in another death.

CHRISTINE LAHTI

2416 Benjamin Avenue
GPS Coordinates: 42.50998, -83.17395

Though Birmingham claims her as their own—and most sources cite Christine Lahti's birthplace as Birmingham—this is simply not true. Even she has said in interviews that she was actually born in Royal Oak and lived there until the age of eight. Her Beaumont Hospital surgeon father moved the family to Birmingham in 1958. There, she graduated from Seaholm High School and then attended University of Michigan. Her lauded career includes an Oscar nomination as Best Supporting Actress in Goldie Hawn's *Swing Shift*; an Oscar win for starring in and directing the 1995 Best Live Action Short, *Lieberman in Love*; and an Emmy Award for her starring role in TV's *Chicago Hope*. That role also won her a 1998 Golden Globe and a trip to the podium, which she was famously late to. She explained to a national TV audience in her acceptance speech, "I was in the bathroom, Mom!"

2416 Benjamin Street, located east of Woodward Avenue, between 12 and 13 Mile Roads.

SOUTHFIELD

SELMA BLAIR

22445 Coventry Woods Lane
GPS Coordinates: 42.49300, -83.26647

Drop the last name of former Southfield resident Selma Blair Beitner, and you have current Hollywood resident Selma Blair. But she didn't drop her name because it sounded more movie-starrish; she and her sister dropped their last name because, after her parents divorced, Selma's father's girlfriend tried to derail her career. Because of this, she also didn't speak to her father for twelve years. Blair went to Hillel Day School in Farmington Hills, Cranbrook Kingswood and then studied photography for two years at Kalamazoo College. After that, she went to New York University to study photography but came back to Michigan to attend University of Michigan, where she graduated magna cum laude in 1994 with a triple degree for photography, psychology and English. While at Cranbrook, she got a taste of acting, which captured her attention above all other interests. Her big break came on Nickelodeon's *The Adventures of Pete and Pete*, which eventually led her to the movies *Cruel Intentions*, *Legally Blonde* and the *Hellboy* franchise. In 2018, Blair revealed she had multiple sclerosis but continued to act and pen her autobiography, *Mean Baby: A Memoir of Growing Up*.

JAY SEBRING

Holy Sepulchre Catholic Cemetery
25800 West 10 Mile Road
GPS Coordinates: 42.47173, -83.29866

You probably don't know how close you are to one of the people who was in Sharon Tate's house the night of the Manson murders on August 9, 1969. You're six feet from Jay Sebring, who is buried in Holy Sepulchre Catholic Cemetery in Southfield. He was an A-list celebrity hair stylist, the founder of the still-in-business Sebring International and ex-boyfriend of Tate. He grew up in Detroit as Thomas Kummer before he went to Los Angeles,

22445 Coventry Woods Lane, located south of 12 Mile Road, east of Telegraph Road.

Holy Sepulchre Cemetery, 25800 West 10 Mile Road, located west of Telegraph Road, south of I-696. The grave site is located in section 24, lot 281, no. 12, on the west side of cemetery.

where he changed his name (Jay, after the first initial of his middle name, and Sebring after the race car). At the end of Quentin Tarantino's *Once Upon a Time in Hollywood*, the fictional Sebring is the one who meets Rick Dalton in the driveway of Tate's home and brings him up to her house.

MAX WRIGHT

20702 Midway Street
GPS Coordinates: 42.45161, -83.24736

Fairview Cemetery
584 East Broad Street
GPS Coordinates: 42.81472, -83.77238

When the alien star of TV's *ALF* crash-landed on Earth, he arrived in the garage of Willie Tanner, played by Max Wright. George Edward Wright (he changed his name to Max because there was already an actor named George Wright) was born in Detroit but grew up on Midway Street in Southfield. He attended Southfield Senior High School and went to Wayne State University for a short period before he moved to Montreal to study drama at the National Theater School of Canada. *ALF* (Alien Life Force) ran on NBC for four years, from 1986 to 1989, reaching number 10 in the Nielsen ratings in its second season. Relying heavily on puppetry, each thirty-minute episode took twenty to twenty-five hours to shoot, which took a toll on the human actors, including Wright, who couldn't wait for the show to be canceled (he got his wish in 1990). Despite having appearances in *Friends*, *The Norm Show* and the movie *All That Jazz*, Wright couldn't shake his role playing opposite a puppet who got all the good lines. In the early 2000s, headlines involving drug use, alcohol and sex tapes pretty much killed his career. Though he successfully beat lymphoma in 1995, it returned in 2019 and eventually took his life when he was seventy-five years old; at the time, he was living at the Actors Fund Home in Englewood, New Jersey. He is buried in Fairview Cemetery in Linden, Michigan, the home of his mother, who had died earlier that same year.

20702 Midway Street, located west of Evergreen Road, south of 9 Mile Road.

Fairview Cemetery, 584 East Broad Street, located west of U.S. 23 off Silver Lake Road on the right. Go through the entrance and then to the right toward the south side of the cemetery.

ST. CLAIR SHORES

DAVE COULIER

21824 Lange Street
GPS Coordinates: 42.47797, -82.89751

In 1986, stand-up comedian Dave Coulier made the cut as a cast member of *Saturday Night Live*. But before the season kicked off, Coulier was deemed too similar to Dana Carvey and was dropped. But shed no tears for Coulier, because the following year, he was cast as Joey Gladstone in TV's popular *Full House*, which ran from 1986 to 1995 (he also appeared in its reboot, *Fuller House*, from 2016 to 2020). His impressive impersonations and voice work also landed him countless jobs as characters in the world of animation, from Animal and Bunsen on *Muppet Babies* to Peter Venkman on *The Real Ghostbusters*. Coulier grew up here in St. Clair Shores, graduating from Notre Dame High School in 1977. He spent a year at University of Michigan but dropped out to put all his efforts into pursuing a career in comedy.

FRED "SONIC" SMITH AND PATTI SMITH

22501 Beach Street
GPS Coordinates: 42.47782, -82.88546

Mt. Elliott Cemetery
1701 Mt. Elliott Street
GPS Coordinates: 42.35156, -83.01664

On a crest in section V of the historic Elmwood Cemetery is the burial site of legendary MC5 guitarist Fred "Sonic" Smith, the husband of the "Poet of Punk," Patti Smith. After suffering from declining health, Sonic succumbed to heart failure at the age of forty-six. Patti had his headstone made using two stones from the cliff in Ireland where he had proposed to her. They first met in 1976 at Lafayette Coney Island, and before they got married, they lived in the Book Cadillac Hotel. Eventually, the Smiths

21824 Lange Street, located south of 10 Mile Road, west of Jefferson Road.

22501 Beach Street, located north of East 10 Mile Road, east of Jefferson Avenue.

Mt. Elliott Cemetery, 1701 Mt. Elliott Street, located south of East Vernor Highway, north of East Lafayette Street, section V.

moved to this home in St. Clair Shores, where they listened to Detroit Tigers games and records in an unseaworthy Chris-Craft boat they kept in their yard. The boat was their respite until lightning struck the nearby willow tree and it fell on the beached vessel. Their Beach Street home was built on a canal in 1918, a year after Prohibition began in Michigan. It's thought that the home was used to harbor illegal liquor dealings, as there was a secret bookcase door that opened to a winding staircase that led down to a secret room with several cots. The Smith family moved to New York two years after Fred died, but Patti owned the home until 2015. Their guitarist son, Jackson, returned here and lived in the house from 2000 to 2005. Four years later, like his mother and father before him, he married a famous musician, Meg White, the ex-wife of The White Stripes' Jack White. They divorced in 2013.

TROY

JOHN DELOREAN

White Chapel Memorial Cemetery
621 West Long Lake Road
GPS Coordinates: 42.59182, -83.16431

You have to wonder, if it wasn't for the *Back to the Future* films, would a DeLorean have been as easily forgotten as something like a Muntz Jet? Not if its namesake had anything to do with it. Though he made much better muscle cars during his time at GM, the maverick founder of the ill-fated DeLorean Motor Company made sure that his car would not be forgotten, as he had his signature gull-winged albatross put on his tombstone. He died from a stroke at the age of eighty and was buried in the northeastern area of White Chapel Memorial Cemetery.

White Chapel Memorial Cemetery, 621 West Long Lake Road, located east of Crooks Road. The grave site is located through entrance to left, section 4775, block G-2.

WYANDOTTE

LUCILLE BALL

3738 Biddle Avenue
GPS Coordinates: 42.19532, -83.15335

In 1914, there was an apartment home here at 126 Biddle Avenue in Wyandotte (demolished in 1963, the address is now 3738 Biddle Avenue). The back apartment was rented for ten dollars a month to Henry and DeDe Ball and their daughter, Lucille. Yep, Lucille Ball lived here between the ages of about one and three, when her father moved them from Jamestown, New York, to Wyandotte so he could take a job with Bell Telephone Company. In 1915, Henry came down with typhoid fever (supposedly from contaminated ice cream) and died at the age of twenty-six. The body of Lucy's father was sent by train back to Jamestown, along with a pregnant DeDe (with Lucy's brother, Fred) and the future "TV Queen of Comedy."

WALLY COX

28 Eureka Road
GPS Coordinates: 42.20003, -83.14885

Before Woody Allen became the poster child for "nebbish," there was a poster child for "nebbish" named Wally Cox. He was the star of the early '50s TV sitcom *Mr. Peepers*. More people may know him as the occupant of the upper-left square on the original *The Hollywood Squares* game show. And even more may know him (or his voice) as the cartoon character Underdog. As a youngster and the son of divorced parents, he moved around numerous times, including to this apartment in Wyandotte. He lived here with his mystery writer mother (who wrote under the pseudonym Eleanor Blake) and sister. He also lived in Evanston, Illinois, where he met a lifelong and seemingly unlikely friend, Marlon Brando. He later lived in Chicago and New York City and then moved back to Detroit, where he graduated in 1942 from Denby High School, where he was voted "Most Clever" and "Most Intelligent." He died in Hollywood in 1973 of a heart attack at the age of forty-eight.

3738 Biddle Street (originally 126 Biddle Street), located east of Fort Street, north of Emmons Road. (It no longer exists.)

28 Eureka Road, located east of Biddle Street.

LEE MAJORS

766 Clinton Street
GPS Coordinates: 42.22893, -83.16196

Carl Yeary of Wyandotte died in an industrial accident at Great Lakes Steel five months before his wife, Alice, gave birth to their son. She and her son, Harvey Lee Yeary, lived in a home on Clinton Street that was once located between the two homes that now stand on the site, before the neighborhood was rebuilt over the years. Then, just seventeen months after giving birth, Alice was killed while waiting for a bus at Clinton and Biddle Streets by a drunk driver who jumped the curb. Harvey was adopted by his aunt and uncle, who moved him to their home in Middlesboro, Kentucky. That boy grew up to be actor Lee Majors, the star of the *Six Million Dollar Man*, *The Fall Guy* and *The Big Valley*. And as a bonus, he was the husband of *Charlie's Angels* star Farrah Fawcett from 1973 to 1982.

YPSILANTI

IGGY POP

3423 Carpenter Road, lot no. 110
GPS Coordinates: 42.23900, -83.67789

While Motown was doing its thing in Detroit, the Iguanas were doing a whole different thing in Ypsilanti. It was a five-man garage rock band that started as a duo for a high school talent show. Its drummer/vocalist was a guy named Jim Osterberg. Jim started playing drums in the fifth grade and lived in Coachville trailer park. His parents moved out of their bedroom, the largest room in the trailer, to accommodate their son's drum set. In 1965, the Iguanas were one of the most popular bands on the scene, but Osterberg sensed music was changing. He left the band he cofounded to join Prime Movers, with bandmates dubbing him "Iggy," a reference to his former group. He began attending college at the school where he first played fraternity parties, University of Michigan, but dropped out to continue his music quest. He then formed the Psychedelic Stooges. (It was later just the

Above: 766 Clinton Street, located south of Emmons Street, east of Fort Street. (It was located between these two homes, but it no longer exists.)

Left: 3423 Carpenter Road, located east of U.S. 23, north of East Ellsworth Road, lot no. 110.

Stooges, after guitarist Ron Asheton called Moe Howard and asked him if he'd mind the shortened name, to which Moe responded, "I don't care what you call yourselves, as long as it's not *The Three Stooges*.") These bandmates gave Osterberg another nickname, Pop, after Jim Popp, a colorful local character Iggy reminded them of. This band also exploded on the scene, with Pop's Jim Morrison/Mick Jagger/James Brown stage persona a favorite of the crowd. Many highs and lows followed, including Pop's heroin addiction (which he eventually beat); a long, successful collaboration with David Bowie (they cowrote the hit "China Girl," among others); a brilliant solo career (*Lust for Life*); reunions (Stooges at Coachella in 2003); acting (as James Mecklenberg in *The Adventures of Pete & Pete*); soundtracks (*Trainspotting*); voice work (*Grand Theft Auto IV*); and awards (a *Lifetime Achievement Grammy*). Now in his seventies, Iggy Pop lives in Miami, a city he calls "a sunny place with shady people."

BIBLIOGRAPHY

General Sources

Ancestry. www.ancestry.com.
Biography. www.biography.com.
Detroit Free Press. www.freep.com.
Detroit Historical Society. www.detroithistorical.org.
Detroit the Way We Remember It. www.facebook.com/groups/376600343614281.
Detroit White Pages
Encyclopedia.com. www.encyclopedia.com.
Encyclopaedia Brittanica. www.brittanica.com.
Historic Boston-Edison. www.historicbostonedison.org.
IMDB. www.imdb.com.
99.1 WFMK. www.99wfmk.com.
Pinterest. www.pinterest.com.
Quora. www.quora.com.
Seaholm High School. www.seaholm.birmingham.k12.mi.us.
United States Census
Wayne State University. www.cfpca.wayne.edu/alumni/directory.
Why Don't We Own This? https://www.tumblr.com/wdwot/33161869226/73-former-detroit-celebrity-homes-the-500.
Wikipedia. www.wikipedia.org.
Woodlawn Cemetery. www.woodlawncemeterydetroit.com/notable-lives.

Chapter 1

Fitzgerald, Natalie. "Della Reese (1931–2017)." Black Past. October 28, 2018. https://www.blackpast.org/african-american-history/reese-della-1931-2017/.

McMahon, Ed. *Here's Ed: The Autobiography of Ed McMahon*. New York: Putnam, 1976.

Chapter 2

Cox, John. "The Last Look at Houdini on Earth." Wild About Houdini. August 26, 2014. https://www.wildabouthoudini.com/2014/08/the-last-look-at-houdini-on-earth.html.

Historic Detroit. www.historicdetroit.org.

NBC News. "Casey Kasem to Be Buried in Norway." August 15, 2014. https://www.nbcnews.com/pop-culture/celebrity/casey-kasem-be-buried-norway-because-its-heaven-n181626.

Rynearson, Jan. "Kasem Tells Tale of His Fenton Roots." Myfenton.com. March 29, 2008. https://www.tctimes.com/kasem-tells-tale-of-his-fenton-roots/article_fbba93ca-e468-51d3-afdd-c950dd4ce044.html.

Wong Barnstead, Elizabeth. "A Prayer in Detroit: Danny Thomas and the Saint of Hopeless Causes." *Detroit Catholic*, May 1, 2015. https://www.detroitcatholic.com/news/a-prayer-in-detroit-danny-thomas-and-the-saint-of-hopeless-causes.

Chapter 3

Kasic, Janet. "*Grand Torino*." Michigan Film and Digital Media Office. www.michiganbusiness.org/499486/globalassets/documents/film/final_gran_torino_tour.pdf.

Kuras, Amy. "The Hidden Treasures of Detroit Public Library's Special Collections." *Model D*, March 1, 2016. https://www.modeldmedia.com/features/hidden-treasures-detroit-public-library-030116.aspx.

Quora. "The Miracles Became Smokey Robinson & the Miracles?" June 27, 2019. https://www.quora.com/The-Miracles-became-Smokey-Robinson-The-Miracles-after-the-release-of-Mickeys-Monkey-Why-did-they-change.

Uitti, Jacob. "Behind Chris Cornell's Death and Conspiracy Theories." *American Songwriter*, 2023. https://americansongwriter.com/behind-chris-cornells-death-and-conspiracy-theories/.

Chapter 4

Bethencourt, Daniel. "Skateboarding Legend Tony Hawk Buys Home in Detroit's Woodbridge Area." *Detroit Free Press*, August 24, 2016.

Bulanda, George. "The Way It Was—Trumbull General Hospital, 1967." *Hour Detroit*, May 30, 2023. https://www.hourdetroit.com/the-way-it-was-articles/the-way-it-was-trumbull-general-hospital-1967/.

Leerhsen, Charles. *Ty Cobb: A Terrible Beauty.* New York: Simon & Schuster, 2016.

RadioX. "The Truth About Jack and Meg White." March 30, 2024. https://www.radiox.co.uk/artists/white-stripes/story-jack-and-meg-white-origins-marriage-split/.

Tallturtle82. "Jack White: Childhood/Early White Stripes Home." virtualglobetrotting. December 23, 2014.

virtualglobetrotting. "Jack White—Childood/Early White Stripes Home." https://virtualglobetrotting.com/map/jack-white-childhood-early-white-stripes-home/view/google/.

Chapter 5

Archie, Trinity. "Lizzo's Life from Childhood to Stardom." Nicki Swift. November 3, 2022. https://www.nickiswift.com/1085333/lizzos-life-from-childhood-to-stardom/.

Letterman, David. "Lizzo." *My Next Guest Needs No Introduction with David Letterman*. Directed by Helen M. Cho. Los Gatos, CA: Netflix, October 21, 2020.

Velarde, Liv. "Lizzo's Home Will Always Be Detroit." Narcity Detroit. November 27, 2019. https://www.narcity.com/detroit/where-lizzo-is-from-is-detroit-michigan-and-her-childhood-is-super-relatable

Chapter 6

Adoptions with Love. "Keegan-Michael Key's Adoption Story." July 23, 2020. https://adoptionswithlove.org/uncategorized/uncategorized-keegan-michael-key-adoption-story.

Atlanta Journal-Constitution. "Michael Jackson Memorial Buried in Detroit." https://www.ajc.com/entertainment/music/michael-jackson-memorial-buried-detroit/MNJUOp8SXzoxUkALnEFLZP/#:~:text=IN%20A%20somewhat%20macabre%20ceremony,mementos%20dedicated%20to%20Michael%20Jackson.

Black Detroiters, @blackdetroiters. Post from May 28, 2023. Instagram. https://www.instagram.com/p/Csy9rdfOYuc/.

Brogan, Tom. "Fourteen Interesting Facts About Harold and Maude." Medium. January 30, 2021. https://tombrogan.medium.com/fourteen-interesting-facts-about-harold-and-maude-9ae5c928290d.

Campione, Katie. "Big Sean Says He Grew 2 Inches Taller This Year by Going to the Chiropractor." *People*, August 3, 2021. https://people.com/music/big-sean-taller-this-year-going-to-the-chiropractor/#:~:text=The%20%22Bounce%20Back%22%20rapper%2C,t%20come%20from%20his%20stature.&text=%22People%20think%20it's%20for%20all,mentor%2C%20his%20name%20was%20Sean.

Canfield, David. "David Alan Grier Always Knew He Could Do It All." *Vanity Fair*, April 14, 2023. https://www.vanityfair.com/hollywood/2023/04/david-alan-grier-always-great-the-patient-awards-insider.

Carl V. "The Redford Theatre: Classic Movies in a Classic Movie House." Tripadvisor. July 2, 2014. https://www.tripadvisor.com/ShowUserReviews-g42139-d2547116-r213279310-The_Redford_Theatre-Detroit_Michigan.html.

Carter, Richard G. "Remembering the Temptations' Late, Great Controversial David Ruffin." *Shepherd Express*, January 18, 2022. https://shepherdexpress.com/music/music-feature/remembering-the-temptations-late-great-controversial-david-r/.

Celebrity Net Worth. "Roger Corman." June 24, 2024. https://www.celebritynetworth.com/richest-businessmen/producers/roger-corman-net-worth/.

Discuss Detroit. "Famous People and Their Detroit Connections." 2007. https://www.atdetroit.net/forum/messages/91697/103603.html?1182415248.

Foley, Aaron. "Mary Wilson's Detroit Story, Unfiltered." The Neighborhoods, City of Detroit. https://theneighborhoods.org/story/mary-wilsons-detroit-story-unfiltered.

Gross, Terry. "David Alan Grier's 'Sporting Life' On Broadway." NPR. May 22, 2012. https://www.npr.org/transcripts/152848779?storyId=152848779.

Gumby World. "Art on the Art of Film and Animation." https://www.gumbyworld.com/art-clokey/art-on-art-of-film-and-animation/.

Henry Ford College. "HFC Alumnus Tom Skerritt: 'It's All About the Storytelling.'" January 19, 2018. https://www.hfcc.edu/news/2018/hfc-alumnus-tom-skerritt-its-all-about-storytelling.

Hopper, Alex. "The Story Behind the Murder of Marvin Gaye." *American Songwriter*, April 1, 2023. https://americansongwriter.com/the-story-behind-the-murder-of-marvin-gaye/.

Jacobs, Hal. "Gladys Knight." *New Georgia Encyclopedia*. April 8, 2021. https://www.georgiaencyclopedia.org/articles/arts-culture/gladys-knight-b-1944/#:~:text=Knight%20was%20born%20on%20May,group%2C%20from%201950%20to%201953.

Kavanagh, Karina. "35 Facts About David Alan Grier." FACTS.net. June 2, 2024. https://facts.net/celebrity/35-facts-about-david-alan-grier/#google_vignette.

Kelly, Leonard. "An Evening with Keegan-Michael Key and Elle Key." Chicago Humanities Festival. December 19, 2023. https://www.youtube.com/watch?v=e_zyDpbNipg.

Lehmer, Larry. "Dinah Washington, 'Queen of the Blues,' Dead at Age 39." *Before Their Time*. January 17, 2013. https://whenwordsmatter.typepad.com/before_their_time/2013/01/dinah-washington-was-looking-forward-to-christmas-after-six-weeks-out-west-singing-for-adoring-audiences-in-los-angeles-an.html.

martakristen.com. "Disney Newcomer Marta Kristen Has Real-Life Cinderella Story." http://www.martakristen.com/marta/film/sam/sampr/sampr02.html.

Military.com. "Famous Veteran: Roger Corman." April 2, 2013. https://www.military.com/veteran-jobs/career-advice/military-transition/famous-veteran-roger-corman.html.

Raven, Benjamin. "Joe Louis' House in Detroit's Historic Boston-Edison Neighborhood Sells." MLive. December 30, 2016. https://www.mlive.com/news/detroit/2016/12/joe_louis_house_in_detroits_hi.html.

Ryan Mendoza. "Rosa Parks Family Home." https://ryan-mendoza.com/rosa%20parks%20family%20home.

Schollenberger, Katrina. "Lots of Love: Who Are Keegan-Michael Key's Parents and Was He Adopted?" *U.S. Sun*, October 4, 2023. https://www.the-sun.com/entertainment/2897716/keegan-michael-key-adoptive-parents/.

Steinberg, Stephanie. "Courtney B. Vance Reflects on Detroit Country Day Years." *Detroit News*, September 17, 2016. https://www.detroitnews.com/story/entertainment/television/2016/09/17/actor-courtney-vance-reflects-years-detroit-country-day/90519310/.

TheFamousPeople. "Robert Wagner Biography." https://www.thefamouspeople.com/profiles/robert-wagner-31364.php.

Time. "George C. Scott: Tempering a Terrible Fire." March 22, 1971. https://content.time.com/time/subscriber/article/0,33009,904935-4,00.html.

Wagmeister, Elizabeth. "R. Kelly Silenced Aaliyah and Her Family with Non-Disclosure Agreement After Marriage Annulment, Docuseries Reveals." *Variety*, January 3, 2023. "https://variety.com/2023/music/news/r-kelly-aaliyah-nda-marriage-annulment-1235478393/.

We Are the Independents. "Keegan-Michael Key's Path to Stardom Began at University of Detroit Mercy." July 17. https://wearetheindependents.com/2015/07/17/keegan-michael-keys-path-to-stardom-began-at-university-of-detroit-mercy/.

Chapter 7

WXYZ-TV. "Eminem Sells 700 Bricks from His Childhood Home." May 24, 2016. https://www.wxyz.com/news/region/detroit/eminem-quickly-sells-700-bricks-from-his-childhood-home-in-detroit-they-came-with-a-casette-tape#:~:text=Eminem%20put%20the%20bricks%20up,LP%2C%20and%20its%20sequel.%22.

Chapter 8

Allen Ginsberg Project. "Edith Parker Kerouac." October 29, 2023. https://allenginsberg.org/2023/10/s-o29-edith-parker-kerouac/.

Anderson, Matt. "The Henry Ford and *National Lampoon's Vacation*." The Henry Ford. May 1, 2019. https://www.thehenryford.org/explore/blog/the-henry-ford-and-national-lampoon's-vacation.

Bertinelli, Valerie. "#tbt Clarkston, Michigan 1971." Facebook post, August 11, 2016. https://www.facebook.com/WolfiesMom/photos/tbt-clarkston-michigan-1971-/963656243745535/?paipv=0&eav=AfYb_wSUVXrH9qR6svH9QP-D-r-wp93wr5wpKOZVrYtJkgHMx6UxjoyfeciEj4WQHCk&_rdr.

Black, Ariel. "'Say Nice Things About Detroit' Creator Helps Carry on Message." Crain's Detroit Business. August 26, 2015. https://www.crainsdetroit.com/article/20150826/NEWS/150829890/say-nice-things-about-detroit-creator-helps-carry-on-message.

Bloomfield Historical Society. "Stonycroft (Theodore F. MacManus) 1920–1960." https://www.bloomfieldhistoricalsociety.org/53-stoneycroft-1920-1960/.

Brody, Lisa, and R.J. King. "The Business of Rock." *DBusiness*, October 21, 2009. https://www.dbusiness.com/business-features/the-business-of-rock/.

CNN. "Bidding on Madonna's Childhood Home." May 25, 2012. https://www.youtube.com/watch?v=yq61SbIJFTw.

Cohassey, John. "Winter of His Discontent." *Detroit Metro Times*, January 20, 2010. https://www.metrotimes.com/arts/winter-of-his-discontent-2196683.

Davids, Judy. "Royal Oak Remembers Jack Kevorkian." Patch. June 5, 2011. https://patch.com/michigan/royaloak/royal-oak-remembers-jack-kevorkian.

Doelle, Katie. "Historical Architecture of Grosse Pointe—15410, Windmill Pointe." July 8, 2014. https://katiedoelle.com/historical-architecture-of-grosse-pointe-15410-windmill-pointe/.

Encyclopedia of World Biography. "Kristen Bell Biography." https://www.notablebiographies.com/news/A-Ca/Bell-Kristen.html.

Find a Grave. "Fred 'Sonic' Smith." https://www.findagrave.com/memorial/7127269/fred-smith.

Gladstone, Doug. "Curtis Armstrong: Oakland University Grad Comes Home." *Jewish News*, July 11, 2023. https://www.thejewishnews.com/culture/arts/curtis-armstrong-oakland-university-grad-comes-home/article_a10c5d90-1f37-11ee-82b9-0b0c039eab3a.html.

Goodwillie, Ian. "*Home Improvement*: 10 Hidden Details You Never Noticed About the Taylors' House." ScreenRant. April 11, 2020. https://screenrant.com/home-improvement-taylors-house-hidden-details/#car-toys-everywhere.

Graff, Gary. "Life on 'The Farm.'" *Oakland Press*, October 11, 2009. http://www.colini.com/Segersfarm.htm.

Hollywood Reporter. "Read John Hughes' Original *National Lampoon* Vacation Story That Started the Movie Franchise." July 29, 2015. https://www.hollywoodreporter.com/movies/movie-features/read-john-hughes-original-national-811591/.

Infoplease. "Chad Everett." https://www.infoplease.com/people/who2-biography/chad-everett.

Jewish Virtual Library. "Selma Blair." https://www.jewishvirtuallibrary.org/selma-blair.

Johnson, Gary. "Marshall Crenshaw." Michigan Rock and Roll Hall of Fame. June 1, 2014. https://michiganrockandrolllegends.com/index.php/mrrl-hall-of-fame/352-marshall-crenshaw.

Karr, Todd. "Robin Williams Visits Country Day." *Day Times*, May/June 1982.

Kennedy Center. "Julie Harris." https://www.kennedy-center.org/artists/h/ha-hn/julie-harris/.

Klug, Emma. "Dave Coulier Trades Hollywood for Hometown of Metro Detroit." *Hour Detroit*, September 4, 2019. https://www.hourdetroit.com/art-and-entertainment/dave-coulier-detroit-full-house-lake-st-clair/.

Leonard, Elmore. "How I Write." *GQ*, August 19, 2013. https://www.gq.com/story/elmore-leonard-how-to-write.

Loria, Keith. "Someday Is Now for Marshall Crenshaw." *Tysons Premier*, January 4, 2016. http://vivatysons.com/blog/2016/01/04/someday-is-now-for-marshall-crenshaw/.

McMurtrie, Layla. "Singer Anita Baker Is Selling Her Grosse Pointe Mansion—But It's a Fixer-Upper." *Detroit Metro Times*, November 21, 2023. https://www.metrotimes.com/detroit/singer-anita-baker-is-selling-her-grosse-pointe-mansion-but-its-a-fixer-upper/Slideshow/34683983.

Monroe City Directory. N.p., 1954.

nailhed. "Lions and Tigers and Beatniks, Oh My." https://www.nailhed.com/2014/10/lions-and-tigers-and-beatniks-oh-my.html.

Page, Maxine. "The Sad Truth About Tim Allen's Childhood." Nicki Swift. September 25, 2023. https://www.nickiswift.com/1402657/sad-truth-tim-allen-childhood/.

Prabook. "Wallace Maynard Cox." https://prabook.com/web/wallace.cox/3761037.

Samoray, Jeff. "Joni Doesn't Live Here Anymore." *Detroit News*, September 16, 1977. https://jonimitchell.com/library/view.cfm?id=647.

Shepard, Dax. "Laura LaBo." *Armchair Expert*. July 2018. https://armchairexpertpod.com/.

Showbiz CheatSheet. "Dax Shepard's Name Was Actually Inspired by a Famous Book Character." September 9, 2021. https://www.cheatsheet.com/entertainment/dax-shepard-name-was-actually-inspired-by-famous-book-character.html/.

Smith, Patti. "A Love Supreme." September 23, 2023. https://pattismith.substack.com/p/a-love-supreme.

TheFamousPeople. "Wally Cox Biography." https://www.thefamouspeople.com/profiles/wally-cox-44334.php.

Township of Independence

Township of West Bloomfield

Tudtud, Christell Fatima M. "Kristen Bell's Mother Lorelei Frygier Was a Nurse with Dark Sense of Humor." AmoMama. March 7, 2023. https://news.amomama.com/400228-kristen-bells-mother-lorelei-frygier-was.html.

Tutton, Mark. "Iggy Pop: 'I Was Looking for an Elegant Coma.'" CNN. https://www.cnn.com/2008/TRAVEL/12/03/iggy.interview.miami/index.html#:~:text=CNN%3A%20What%20made%20you%20move,lot%20of%20peace%20and%20convenience.

Vogel, Elizabeth. "Jack Kerouac's Brief Interlude in Grosse Pointe." Patch. March 13, 2011. https://patch.com/michigan/grossepointe/jack-kerouacs-brief-interlude-in-grosse-pointe.

Whitworth, Elizabeth. "Why Did Malcolm X Change His Name-Twice?" Shortform. August 31, 2023. https://www.shortform.com/blog/why-did-malcolm-x-change-his-name/.

WorthPoint. "Denby High School Yearbook 1942 Wally Cox." https://www.worthpoint.com/worthopedia/denby-high-school-year-book-1942-19984567.

ABOUT THE AUTHOR

Steve Platto grew up at 30960 Roycroft Street, Livonia, Michigan, where he first got the writing bug by creating one-act plays he forced his friends to be in at Buchanan Elementary School. As a teen, he developed a voracious love for reading...*Mad* magazine. He also made Super 8 movies, memorized copious amounts of useless pop culture trivia and, in college, drew humorous editorial cartoons for the university newspaper until he wore his pencils down to nubs. This all laid the groundwork for him to become an advertising agency group creative director/writer, a career he has enjoyed over the last thirty-five-plus years. Today, he and his wife, Cris, live in Royal Oak—half a mile from the former apartment of Dr. Jack Kevorkian.